M000310308

The Cross Examen

The Cross Examen

— *A Spirituality for Activists* —

Roger J. Gench

CASCADE *Books* • Eugene, Oregon

THE CROSS EXAMEN
A Spirituality for Activists

Copyright © 2020 Roger J. Gench. All rights reserved. Except for brief
quotations in critical publications or reviews, no part of this book may
be reproduced in any manner without prior written permission from the
publisher. Write: Permissions, Wipf and Stock Publishers, 199 W. 8th Ave.,
Suite 3, Eugene, OR 97401.

Cascade Books
An Imprint of Wipf and Stock Publishers
199 W. 8th Ave., Suite 3
Eugene, OR 97401

www.wipfandstock.com

PAPERBACK ISBN: 978-1-5326-8836-2
HARDCOVER ISBN: 978-1-5326-8837-9
EBOOK ISBN: 978-1-5326-8838-6

Cataloguing-in-Publication data:

Names: Gench, Roger J., author.

Title: The cross examen : a spirituality for activists / Roger J. Gench.

Description: Eugene, OR: Cascade Books, 2020 | Includes bibliographi-
cal references.

Identifiers: ISBN 978-1-5326-8836-2 (paperback) | ISBN 978-1-5326-
8837-9 (hardcover) | ISBN 978-1-5326-8838-6 (ebook)

Subjects: LCSH: Bible. Galatians—Criticism, interpretation, etc. | Politi-
cal theology. | Atonement.

Classification: BS2685.2 .G50 2020 (print) | BS2685.2 (ebook)

Manufactured in the U.S.A.   10/23/20

Contents

CONTENTS

Acknowledgments

FOR OVER THIRTY YEARS, in varied urban church settings, I have explored intersections between the academic guild and the practices of ministry. These explorations are reflected in this book and have been at the heart and core of my ministry.

I am indebted to a number of groups, institutions, congregations, and individuals with whom I have engaged material in this volume as it has taken shape and for conversations that have left significant marks upon it. Initial drafts of my reflection on the Cross Examen and the Spirituality of the Cross were presented at the Summer Institute for Pastors at the Lutheran Theological Seminary in Gettysburg, Pennsylvania in 2015. I am also grateful to Union Presbyterian Seminary in Virginia for a variety of opportunities to explore this material: in an urban ministry course and an elective course ("Cross Examinations"), both co-taught with Frances Taylor Gench; as the Dawe Lecturer in 2021 on "Cruciform Mindfulness"; and on several occasions as a guest lecturer on Galatians, Pauline spirituality, and the practice of ministry in the New Testament II core course.

I have benefited from leading workshops at NEXT Church Annual Conferences (Presbyterian Church USA) on "The Cross Examen" (2016) and "The Fruit of the Spirit as Political Virtues" (2017)—the latter co-led with my former colleague in ministry, Rev. Alice Rose Tewell. I have also utilized material from this book at NEXT Church Community Organizing Training events in Baltimore in 2017 and 2018 and as a distance educator supervising

ACKNOWLEDGMENTS

the work of cohorts that met monthly in 2018 and 2019 for online conversation and learning.

I am deeply indebted to a collegial reading group of fellow ethicists: Doug Ottati (Davidson College), Elizabeth Hinson-Hasty (Bellarmine University), Mark Douglas (Columbia Theological Seminary), and James Calvin Davis (Middlebury College). They read and commented on drafts of this project, and their insights have been invaluable. I also thank Drs. James Taneti and Nelson Reveley for conversations on early drafts of this book.

I am grateful to various congregations that have provided opportunities for Christian education classes or events focused on the subject matter of this book: Lexington Presbyterian Church in Lexington, Virginia hosted a weekend event addressing racism and the theology of the cross; West Raleigh Presbyterian Church in Raleigh, North Carolina and Christ Presbyterian Church in Camp Hill, Pennsylvania also hosted sessions and discussions from which I benefited. I thank the leadership and members of these churches for their generous hospitality and rich conversation.

Of course, one congregation in particular, The New York Avenue Presbyterian Church in Washington DC, has deeply informed every aspect of this volume, as it was my enormous privilege to serve as senior pastor of this vibrant urban congregation from 2002 to 2019. Throughout the Fall of 2016, I co-taught with Frances Taylor Gench a series of adult Sunday School classes on "Re-politicizing Paul: Fruit of the Spirit for a Contentious, Polarized World." At the same time, I preached a sermon series that explored "The Fruit of the Spirit as Political Virtues." This series began to shape the core material of the book's chapters on the fruit of the Spirit. I want to thank the young adult group of The New York Avenue Presbyterian Church for challenging conversations on the theology of the cross during our monthly Faith on Tap sessions. I also used early drafts of this book with The Engaged Spirituality Group of NYAPC's McClendon Scholar in Residence Program, which met monthly from the fall of 2016 through the summer of 2017. Stories of urban ministry in my former congregation, Brown Memorial Park Avenue Presbyterian Church in

Baltimore, are also reflected in this volume. And I am currently grateful for ongoing engagement with the subject matter of this volume with Rev. Alex Evans and the good people of Second Presbyterian Church in Richmond, Virginia where I currently serve as Theologian in Residence.

I thank Rodney Clapp, my editor at Cascade Books, for inviting me to submit this work for publication and for invaluable editorial assistance leading toward publication.

Finally, I am forever grateful to my spouse, Frances Taylor Gench, for ongoing conversations about the subject matter of every chapter of this book and for generous editorial expertise.

Introduction

IN THE EARLY 1990S, I "hit the wall" in ministry. The local parish I was serving was very demanding—an activist congregation that pulled me in so many different directions that I found myself overwhelmed and shutting down. I knew that I either had to make some changes or leave ministry altogether. So, with a couple of clergy friends, I began a program in spiritual direction designed to equip us to become spiritual directors. The truth is, I had little yearning to become a spiritual director, but I did want to learn how to pray. So, for the next few years, I became a student of the contemplative arts—arts that in many respects saved my ministry and my life! Indeed, for the last twenty-six years, I have been a devotee and teacher of spiritual disciplines. But over time I found that something important was missing—a deep connection between my activism and my spirituality. My spiritual teachers, to be sure, had encouraged engagement with the world, but they did not draw a robust connection between contemplation and activism—the latter was more of an addendum than something integral to the practice of the former. Likewise, in my activist pursuits and circles, there was little discussion of the connection between the inward and outward aspects of our endeavors—spiritual disciplines, if noted at all, were an add-on rather than a crucial aspect of the Christian life of engagement with the world. I sensed a disconcerting disconnect between two important dimensions of my life.

The ground beneath me began to shift when I first encountered Thich Nhat Hanh's extraordinary book *The Miracle of Mindfulness*. I was surprised to learn that this much beloved book on the contemplative art of mindful living was originally addressed to his fellow Buddhist monks in Vietnam at a time when they were deeply engaged in helping peasants rebuild their lives in the wake of the calamitous Vietnam War. They established schools, helped reconstruct bombed villages, and set up medical clinics and agricultural co-ops. They were often persecuted for these activities because they were suspected of alignment with one side or the other in that conflict—though they steadfastly refused to support violence on either side.[1] This book made a deep and lasting impression upon me. Intrigued by the connection between Buddhist mindfulness and activism that Hanh was articulating, I began to explore a Christian counterpart. This book is an exploration of these connections.

Thus, in what follows, I highlight two crucial dimensions of faithful Christian practice that are far too often seen as separate endeavors: spirituality and engagement with the world. Spirituality appeals to many Christians who delve into contemplative practice as a means toward healing and wholeness; others view engagement with the world as the preeminent sign of authentic Christian faith and practice. In my view, both spirituality and engagement with the world are essential and integrally related Christian disciplines. In the pages that follow I invite you to explore their essential relationship—and a point of deep and profound connection between the two. In my own journey of faith, my spirituality and my activism finally came together at an oft-neglected place I had not anticipated at the outset: at the cross of Jesus Christ. So, the book also invites you to ponder the integral connection between spirituality and activism in conversation with the theology of the cross. As we will see, the cross of Jesus Christ reveals both the brokenness in our lives and the corresponding brokenness in the world; it also discloses the God who is always (and already) bringing resurrection and life out of the death-tending ways of our world. The cross and resurrection of Jesus Christ, I contend, expose other crosses, large and small, that litter the landscape of our world and of our personal and corporate lives, as well as places where God's resurrecting power is at work,

1. Hanh, *The Miracle of Mindfulness*, vii–viii.

bringing life out of death and establishing footholds for the unfolding of the new creation. As spirituality and activism finally began to find deeper and essential connection in my own life of faith in the theology and spirituality of the cross, I found the Apostle Paul to be an important and stimulating conversation partner—particularly his letter to the churches in Galatia, where his own theology of the cross finds profound expression. Thus, we will also consider Paul's Letter to the Galatians as a key source of insight for us today. Perhaps it needs to be noted that, for some readers, two key subjects in this book—the cross and the Apostle Paul—instinctively evoke suspicious reactions. Both present obstacles because of traditional, yet deeply problematic, interpretations of them. However, we will engage new angles of vision on the cross and the Apostle Paul that I hope will expand and enliven reflection on both as profound and generative resources for contemporary faith and practice.

In sum, in the chapters that follow, we will consider both contemplative and activist practices that ground authentic Christian engagement with the world. My chief aim in this book is to develop a spirituality of the cross that reveals the places in our lives, in our faith communities, and in the life of the world where God's resurrection power is at work bringing life out of death. In Galatians 6:17, the Apostle Paul maintains, "I carry the marks of Jesus branded on my body." The marks to which he refers are those of crucifixion and resurrection, and I am now convinced that, for Paul, these marks have both personal and political dimensions.

Theologian Kristine Culp, in her own reflection on the theology of the cross, tells an arresting story of meeting a former gang member in Los Angeles who had unusual marks upon him: the word "Florence" was tattooed across his forehead, over his skull, and around his neck. The tattoos defined him as belonging to a particular neighborhood with this name—one ruled by his gang—and carried the threat of violence against anyone who would disrespect it. Culp met this heavily marked man at an agency that aids people trying to escape LA's violent gang culture. Through the ministry of Rev. Gregory Boyle and Homeboy Industries, he had found an alternative culture of justice-seeking love and forgiveness that was helping him reconstruct his life. As a result, this former gang member was literally changing the marks upon him: he was in the midst of the painful process of tattoo removal which required "months of treatment and entailed what are essentially second-degree burns."[2] This story strikes me as an apt metaphor for the human condition, for we all bear the marks of violence upon us—perhaps not physically, but spiritually—for as we will see, the same violence that crucified Jesus crucifies every one of us. But God in Christ is always at work, seeking to bring life out of death, to heal our wounds, and to resurrect us from the death-tending ways of the world, inviting our participation in the divine cosmic restoration project.

Kristine Culp is right on spot when she contends that any reinterpretation of the cross must name suffering as suffering and "unmask brutality, tyranny and indignity." Or as Martin Luther put it, a theology of the cross requires that we "call a thing what it actually is." Culp further contends that a theology of the cross requires theological discernment of how God can bring transformation at the site of violent suffering.[3] I find Culp's interpretation of the cross compelling. So, let me be clear about my own theology of the cross from the outset, as I reject some traditional interpretations of it: I affirm that *suffering due to violence is never redemptive*, as some traditional interpretations of the cross presume. Suffering must be named as suffering. Suffering and violence are an affront to human flourishing and not the will of God. Persecution and pain may be an inevitable result of resistance to suffering and to the powers that inflict it—and this is the cross that disciples of Jesus are called to bear (Mark 8:34)—pain that may come their way as a consequence of their discipleship, of embodying God's will and way in the world. But that is very different from valorizing suffering.[4] I believe that our most basic Christian confession—affirmation of the death and resurrection of Jesus Christ—declares that God, in the crucified and risen Christ, exposes all dehumanizing power that inflicts

2. Culp, *Vulnerability and Glory*, 117, 120.
3. Culp, *Vulnerability and Glory*, 118.
4. See St. Clair, *Call and Consequences*, 23–30, 68.

violence (spiritual, physical, or both) as the antithesis of God—as *not* the way of God in the world—and empowers resistance and transformation at the very site of the abuses.

In the pages that follow, we will engage practices that help us to discern the marks of crucifixion upon us and upon the world, and also the places where God is at work, bringing forth justice, reconciliation, forgiveness, and deeply relational love from all such sites of brokenness. Part I will offer a foundation for engaged or cruciform (cross-shaped) spirituality. Part II will explore Paul's letter to the churches of Galatia as a springboard for reflection on the fruit of the Spirit (Gal 5:22–23) as political virtues for cruciform faith and practice in a polarized and violent world.

Before moving on, let me finally offer a big picture frame for this book that will place in perspective the contribution I hope it can make to a larger project. I affirm that the goal and chief purpose of human life, discipleship, and the church—indeed, of all who belong to the community called to follow Jesus—is to increase love of God and neighbor, as Jesus taught when asked about the greatest commandment: "The first is, 'Hear, O Israel: the Lord our God, the Lord is one; you shall love the Lord your God with all your heart, and with all your soul, and with all your mind, and with all your strength.' The second is this, 'You shall love your neighbor yourself'" (Mark 12:29–31, NRSV). These commandments directly identify an underlying problem of the human condition: our propensity to turn in on ourselves. Though we are created and redeemed in love by the God of the universe to love God and one another and to seek a common life together, we are personally and socially deformed by the love of lesser "gods" (or "not gods," as Paul refers to them in Galatians 4:8; e.g., false gods of prosperity and materialism, of racial and ethnic privileging, of gender exclusivity, of religious bigotry, and of nationalistic imperialism—to mention but a few). Such gods deceive us with the false hope that they will convey us to the "promised land" (the story of the golden calf in Exodus 32:1–14 is instructive in this regard), but they have warped and constricted our vision of who and what we deem worthy of love and justice. As a result, we do violence against those we consider unworthy, and in so doing, we can be described as crucifying them—spiritually and even plainly speaking! Moreover, as we doubt our own worthiness of love, or accept the evaluation of others that we are less than beloved children of God, we do violence to (or crucify) ourselves. *In short, we have been co-opted, hijacked, commandeered, gerrymandered, or, to use biblical imagery, exiled and enslaved, by the false promises of not-gods that warp and crucify us and that incite a "dog-eat-dog," mean-spirited existence.* The great evils/crucifixions of our world are a result of our idolatrous inward turn and the consequent deformation of our hearts, minds, and souls. The cross and resurrection of Jesus, in this context, entail a great awakening that exposes false gods and their violence—the crucifixions large and small all around us—as well as God's radical forgiving, transforming, and justice-seeking love that will not let us go, ever bringing resurrection and new life. The cross/resurrection is an event that draws us out of ourselves towards love of God, neighbor, and self, thereby restoring us to our true human purpose. It is, as N. T. Wright puts it, "the revolution"[5]—the pivotal turning point to which Christians, individually and corporately, always return—one that frees us for resurrection life and participation in God's redemptive activity in the world. So, it is to the cross and resurrection that we now turn.

5. Wright, *The Day*, 4.

Part I

Foundations for Cruciform Spirituality

1

The Spiritual Power of the Cross

> Then the *soldiers led him into the courtyard of the palace (that is, the governor's headquarters)*; they called together the whole cohort. And they clothed him in a purple cloak; and after twisting some thorns into a crown, they put it on him. And they began *saluting* him, *"Hail, King of the Jews!"* They struck his head with a reed, spat upon him, and knelt down in homage to him. After *mocking* him, they stripped him of the purple cloak and put his own clothes on him. Then they led him out to crucify him. . . .
>
> It was nine o'clock in the morning when they crucified him. The inscription of the charge against him read, *"*The King of the Jews." And with him they crucified two bandits, one on his right and one on his left. *Those who passed by derided him, shaking their heads* and saying, "Aha! You who would destroy the temple and build it in three days, save yourself, and come down from the cross!" In the same way the chief priests, along with the scribes, were also *mocking* him among themselves and saying, "He saved others; he cannot save himself. Let the Messiah the King of Israel, come down from the cross now, so that we may see and believe." Those who were crucified with him also *taunted* him. (Mark 15:16–20, 25–32; emphasis mine)

THE CRUCIFIXION OF JESUS, at its base level, was a painful public humiliation—a brutal use of political power intended to draw others into its spell. The Gospel of Mark's account of the crucifixion of Jesus highlights the public and political nature of Jesus' humiliation on the cross in particularly graphic ways, repeatedly emphasizing the political mockery of Jesus: soldiers ridicule him in the courtyard of the governing authority; passersby deride him, shaking their heads at him; religious authorities mock him; and even those crucified with him taunt him. Given the political diminution of Jesus on the cross, it is little wonder that theologian James Cone discerned a correspondence between Jesus' cross and the lynching tree (in a book that bears this title)—as the lynching tree also was and is a public and political symbol of power and denigration.[1]

Paradoxically, just as the early Christians turned the cross, a symbol of Caesar's power, into a symbol of God's unconquered love, Cone points out that the cross, for black people, also came to function as "God's critique of power—white power—with powerless love, snatching victory out of defeat."[2] For Cone, "the cross and the lynching tree represented the worst in human beings and at the same time 'an unquenchable ontological thirst' for life that refuses to let the worst determine our final meaning."[3] In like manner, I would maintain that the cross of Jesus represents the humiliating, dehumanizing abuse of power anywhere and everywhere it is exercised (on however large or small a scale)—a place where such abuse is exposed as *not* the way of God (indeed, as the antithesis of God) in the world, and yet a place where God seeks to bring resurrection, healing, and justice at the very places of brokenness. This is what I call a political theology of the cross—i.e., an understanding of the cross that discerns its exposure of public abuses of power (as well as the personal ramifications of such abuse) embodied in regimes of power, as well as its disclosure of how God in the risen Christ is empowering resurrection (resistance, disruption, and transformation) at the very sites of abuse. Such a theology is grounded in our earliest biblical witnesses, such as the Gospel of Mark's narrative of Jesus' crucifixion, noted above. It is also reflected in the Apostle Paul's understanding of the cross, as we will see. Paul berated the Galatians: "You foolish Galatians! Who has bewitched you? It was

1. Cone, *The Cross*, 7.
2. Cone, *The Cross*, 2.
3. Cone, *The Cross*, 3.

before your eyes that Jesus Christ was publicly exhibited as crucified!" (Gal 3:1). It may seem an odd thing to say to Galatian believers in Asia Minor who were not present in Judea on the occasion
of Jesus' crucifixion; but Pauline scholar Davina Lopez makes an
astute observation about this verse: "Paul's Galatians did not see
Jesus' crucifixion, but they did not have to. There were plenty of
examples before everyone's eyes (in real life, in stone, on coins)
of capture, torture, bondage and execution of others in the name
of affirming Rome's universal sovereignty through domination."[4]
Thus, in Galatians 3:1, Paul gives expression to a political theology
that sees the cross of Jesus as exposing other crosses, large and
small all around us. Theologian Shawn Copeland notes a similar
phenomenon during the era of African American enslavement
wherein the refrain from the spiritual—"Were you there when
they crucified my Lord?"—was intended to confront all who heard
these words with their own complicity in public crucifixions in
their own time and place.[5]

Moreover, a political theology of the cross finds expression in
confessional documents like the Nicene Creed. Indeed, in his fine
introduction to political theology (*Christ and the Common Life*),
theologian Luke Bretherton points out that the inclusion of the
phrase "crucified under Pontus Pilate" in this early creed represents the judgment of God on all local political orders that engage
in tyrannical and exploitative practices. Accordingly, the crucifixion, resurrection, and ascension "expose the limits of their power
and their fear of their own limits. In contrast to Pilate, and in him
all worldly authorities of which he is a type, the resurrection and
ascension unveil the deepest and only life-giving source of power:
the power of the Spirit. The Spirit brings calm out of storms, health
out of disease, and resurrection out of death."[6] In my view, this is
a quintessential expression of the political theology of the cross.
There are, to be sure, myriad ways of understanding the cross and

---

4. Lopez, *Apostle to the Conquered*, 163.
5. Copeland, *Knowing Christ Crucified*, 29–30.
6. Bretherton, *Christ and the Common Life*, 18–20.

resurrection in the Bible and Christian tradition,[7] but a political theology of the cross is a particularly fruitful way of connecting spirituality and engagement with the world, as we will see.

In sum, what do I have in mind when I use the symbol of the cross? Ernest Hemingway once wrote: "The world breaks everyone and afterward many are strong in the broken places."[8] Let me paraphrase Hemingway to define the cross: *The world crucifies everyone, yet God in Christ is always active in the world seeking to bring life out of the broken places.* The cross has two important dimensions: it entails both crucifixion and resurrection, so let me elaborate on each.

Crucifixion

When I speak of crucifixion, I am referring both to a historical reality and also to a symbol for the abuse of power. The historical reality is that Jesus was crucified, and his crucifixion was an instrument of state terrorism that the Roman Empire used to force their subjects into submission.[9] The intention of crucifixion was to break the will of conquered and oppressed peoples and to impose law and order. New Testament scholar Neil Elliott likens Roman crucifixion to the obscene spectacle that government-sponsored death squads made of massive executions during El Salvador's bloody civil war in the 1980s. As he observes, "It was no mere rhetorical flourish when Archbishop Oscar Romero spoke of the 'crucifixion of the Salvadoran people'" by the death squads.[10]

The crucifixion of Jesus, of course, was not an isolated event but rather the result of the kind of life he lived and the kind of ministry he exercised among the crucified—those who in his day (like the Salvadoran campesinos to whom Romero referred) were

7. See, for example, Baker's *Executing God.*

8. Hemingway, *A Farewell to Arms,* 249.

9. I am indebted here to Ted Jennings, who begins his reconstruction of the theology of the cross by emphasizing its historical and public nature. See Jennings, *Transforming Atonement,* 25, 226.

10. Elliott, *Liberating Paul,* 96.

marginalized and subjected to the abuse of power. Biblical scholar Donald Senior observes that Jesus stood with the downtrodden and resisted the forces that oppressed them, and it was because of his life and ministry that he was crucified.[11] Moreover, in each of the Synoptic Gospels, when Jesus teaches his followers that discipleship involves taking up "their cross" (Matt 16:24; Mark 8:34; Luke 9:23), he was not suggesting that they pick up a cross they did not already bear, but rather that they acknowledge and name the crosses bearing down upon their own lives and upon those around them, and resist those savage forces. In other words, crucifixion was (and is) a daily occurrence. Indeed, Luke's version of this saying acknowledges the quotidian nature of crucifixion when Jesus instructs his disciples to "take up their cross *daily*" (Luke 9:23).

In short, crucifixion can be a symbol for the wound of violence and for any exercise of power, however large or small, that dominates, deforms, and defaces human life or God's good creation, for such power mimics the same kind of abusive power that crucified Jesus and those to whom he ministered. Any such exercises of power wound, warp, and crucify. Indeed, as we look at the world through the lens of the cross, it exposes the many crucifixions happening all around us—sites at which human life and God's creation suffer as a result of economic injustice and classism, ethnocentrism and racism, segregation, environmental degradation, sexism, heterosexism, and greed—to name but a few. In each of these cases power crucifies because it is used to dominate, deform, or deface some in order to benefit others, or to keep oppression in place. Moreover, passivity, or the failure to act or speak out in the face of deforming conditions, is itself a kind of crucifying power, because passivity and neglect (sins of omission) enable crucifixions to endure through time. So I use the language of "exposure" or "exposé" to express the symbolic power of the cross of Jesus as a lens that enables us to see other crosses, large and small, that litter both our internal and external landscapes.[12] The cross, in sum, is a symbol for the abuse of power.

11. Senior, *Why the Cross?*, 17.

12. I am indebted to Doug Ottati for this way of describing the effects of

Some may wonder about the legitimacy of using the symbol of the cross for abuses of power, both large and small, in everyday life. Can the cross which, historically speaking, was an horrific and lethal experience of imperial abuse of power for one who died upon it, be used to describe (for example) nonlethal daily experiences of racism, sexism, or homophobia? Good question. If you have ever been on the receiving end of a racist, sexist, homophobic, or exclusionary action, comment, or policy it can surely feel like a wound—akin to the wound of a cross. Those who inflict such wounds may do so unconsciously; but if you are made aware, or conscientized, to the fact that you have inflicted harm through some comment, action, or behavior—or that you have been complicit in a social and cultural world that inflicts harm—it can also be a wounding experience that can lead to shame and remorse, repentance and a search for reparation. To be sure, the wound of the perpetuator and that of the victim differ in nature and degree, but they are woundings nonetheless that disfigure our human experience—and both can be described as crosses, large and small, that disorder and deform our lives.

Psychologist Derald Wing Sue's notion of "microaggression" provides a graphic example of an all too prevalent cross that afflicts many on a daily basis. Sue claims that one of the significant ways minorities (e.g., people of color, women, and gays) are harmed is by well-intentioned people who convey unconscious or barely conscious prejudices, biases that make their way into everyday interactions and practices.[13] He defines microaggressions as brief, everyday "put downs" that denigrate an individual or group because of their race, class, gender, or sexual orientation. For instance, when Asian Americans are praised for speaking proper English or are constantly asked where they are from, the message conveyed is that "you are not American" or "you are a foreigner."[14] Such state-

---

the cross. He contends that through the lens of the cross we "discern the many Calvaries both great and small that clutter the horizons of our world." Ottati, *Jesus Christ*, 87.

13. Sue, *Microaggressions*, xv.

14. Sue, *Microaggressions*, 37.

ments initially might strike one as trivial, but Sue's research shows that a steady barrage of them can affect self-esteem, job performance, and even access to jobs and proper health care. Microaggressions, as Sue observes,

> are a constant and continuing reality for people of color, women, and LBGT's in our society. They hold their power over both perpetrators and targets because of their everyday invisible nature. In many respects, all of us have been both perpetrators and targets. With respect to the former, we have been guilty of having delivered microaggressions, whether they are racial, gender, sexual-orientation, ability, religious, or class based. Microaggressions are harmful to marginalized groups because they cause psychological distress and create disparities in health care, employment, and education.[15]

Microaggressions are but one powerful example of the kinds of crosses that inflict suffering on others.

The cross, then, is a symbol for the abuse of power, large and small. In addition, the theology of the cross of which I speak is grounded in what I call "political theology." For some, *political* is a loaded and problematic word, so let me be clear about my use of it. I am not referring to partisan politics, to red and blue realities (though the cross has implications for such matters). The word *political* comes from the Greek word *polis*, which means "city." As theologian Elizabeth Johnson explains, political theology is "theology that seeks to connect speech about God with the *polis*, the city, the public good of massive numbers of people, living and dead."[16] A political theology of the cross seeks to expose sin that is both public and internalized or inscribed upon us; and it conscientizes us to ways in which we reinscribe sin onto the world around us. In this sense, "political" theology of the cross expands our understanding of its significance, serving as a corrective to notions of the cross that are narrowly focused on the individual.

15. Sue, *Microaggressions*, 39.
16. Johnson, *Quest*, 55.

The notion of inscription deserves special comment because it is illustrative of the way in which sin works and how the cross finds expression in our lives. The prophet Jeremiah perceptively spoke of sin as a reality written on the tablets of human hearts with an iron pen and a diamond stylus (Jer 17:1). The image is that of an engraver carving on stone. Sin, in other words, is deeply etched on our hearts and not easily removed. Think again of the former gang member whose tattoos conveyed the violent rule of the gang in his former neighborhood and in his own life. The tattoos were inscriptions upon his body, and they symbolized the violence he reinscribed on his neighborhood or on other gangs when confrontations arose. Their removal was painful, leaving scars. We may not bear such explicit, visible tattoos of the sin and violence in our lives, but all of us do have similar inscriptions etched on our very hearts.

Another way of thinking about this is conveyed by the profound Korean notion of *han*. *Han*, as theologian Andrew Sung Park explains it, is "a social, economic, political, physical, mental, or spiritual wound generated by political oppression, economic exploitation, social alienation, cultural contempt, injustice, poverty, or war. It may be a deep ache, an intense bitterness, or the sense of helplessness, hopelessness, or resignation at the individual and collective levels."[17] Given the reality of inscription and the deep wounds conveyed by *han*, whenever I conduct an infant or adult baptism, one of the baptismal questions I ask of parent(s) or of the adult baptismal candidate is this: do you renounce evil in the world, that which defies God's justice and love? The vow is an important one, for evil gets inscribed upon us—it is all around us and in the very air we breathe. Racism, sexism, classism, and innumerable other "isms" are in the water and air all around us. They inflict wounds, or crosses, upon our world. We bear their imprint on our hearts and in our lives, and we inevitably reinscribe them on others. In baptism, we affirm that God's love is infinitely more powerful than any inscription—nonetheless, the scars remain. For this reason, it is critical for us to ponder the politics of the cross.

17. Park, *Triune Atonement*, 39.

In his book *Transforming Atonement: A Political Theology of the Cross*, theologian Ted Jennings offers a particularly astute summary of the politics of the cross. The cross, he says, represents a collision between the way of Jesus and the politics of domination. This collision is unavoidable and God's will only in the sense that the roots of suffering and abuse need to be "exposed" and brought to an end.[18] He continues,

> One way that this is expressed in the tradition is that God comes in Christ in order to overcome sin. The end of sin is the end of this game of violence, of collaboration in violence, of imitation of violence—a violence exercised in the name of the supposedly "strong God" it imitates. It is because of "our sin," as Paul suggests, that the Messiah is repudiated, condemned, and executed. *But this does not mean because of a long list of personal sins. It has rather to do with our participation in a world that rules by and collaborates in violence, exclusion, and judgment. This is the pervasive reality in which we are caught up.* It plays out in our relationships with people we "love," as well as in our relationships with our "enemies." It plays out in the relationship of the elite to those they control. But it also plays out among the excluded—not in the same way, but in ways that still mirror the deadly force of domination and division, even when this or that element of oppression is actively opposed. It is this scene of violence and violation that is entered by the messianic mission, and it is from this same dynamic that this mission suffers and dies.[19]

Note the way in which Jennings uses language of "exposure" to speak of the cross. He claims that at its most basic level, the cross "strips the powers of domination and violence of their pretended legitimacy" and reveals God's solidarity with the "oppressed and humiliated."[20] So the cross both "unmasks" and "reveals"—it unmasks domination's pretension to power and reveals God's sovereign and cruciform covenant love.

18. Jennings, *Transforming Atonement*, 214–15.
19. Jennings, *Transforming Atonement*, 215 (emphasis mine).
20. Jennings, *Transforming Atonement*, 61.

In thinking about the cross as "exposure," I recall a conversation with one of my mentors, theologian Douglas Ottati, who suggested that one way of looking at the cross is through the notion of the "right nightmare," drawing on the trilogy of nightmares that afflicted Scrooge in Charles Dickens's *A Christmas Carol*. Scrooge, he noted, did not simply move from miserly to other-regarding behavior through exhortation or mere contact with the down and out. Indeed, Scrooge was a wretched, grasping, covetous man who prized only one virtue: dog-eat-dog lending practices and squeezing every penny out of everyone. He did not pay his lone employee, Bob Cratchit, a decent wage, even though Cratchit's son, Tiny Tim, was sickly. The key to opening Scrooge's heart turns out to be a series of nightmares that "expose" his past, present, and future in the starkest of terms—to the point that he is rendered a sobbing penitent and more than ready to rectify his ways.

The cross actually works in a very similar way. It can be likened to the "right nightmare." The shock of witnessing hideous state-sponsored violence inflicted on the one who stood with the oppressed and embodied the justice-seeking love of the commonwealth of God can awaken the heart and mind to see other crosses (abuses of power) large and small. The Apostle Paul, for example, had just such a dramatic wake-up call on the road to Damascus when confronted by the crucified and risen Christ, asking "Saul, Saul, why do you persecute me?" (Acts 9:1–9; see also Gal 1:13). It was a conversion moment in the sense that from that time on he was no longer a persecutor of the followers of Jesus, but rather a disciple of the crucified and risen Lord. Indeed, in his letter to the Galatian churches he makes an astonishing affirmation: "I have been crucified with Christ; and it is no longer I who live, but it is Christ who lives in me" (Gal 2:19b–20). Paul, like Scrooge, awakened from a nightmare and was able to recognize his participation in the crucifying violence of his world. In fact, as we will see in chapter 3, the whole of Paul's letter to the Galatians can be read as a wake-up call to the reality of the crosses that pervaded their world.

In like manner, the cross of Jesus Christ can awaken us to the violence permeating the world and our own lives. His cross can be discerned in the fate of refugees who drown while fleeing political oppression in unseaworthy boats; in the despair of returning citizens who have paid their debt to society, but are disenfranchised in their search to find work and housing; and in the anguish of undocumented parents torn from their children by ruthless and racist deportation policies. In this sense, the cross functions as the "right nightmare"—we could even call it a "good nightmare," in the same way that we speak, oxymoronically, of "Good Friday." The cross exposes our personal sins with respect to our family and community relations, as the dreams worked on Scrooge, but they also expose our deep interconnections with the inhumanity of our world. As a case in point, Elizabeth Johnson highlights the words of Ignacio Ellacuría, SJ, the martyred president of the University of Central America in San Salvador, addressed to first-world Christians: "I want you to set your eyes and your hearts on these peoples who are suffering so much—some from poverty and hunger, others from oppression and repression. Then (since I am a Jesuit), standing before this people thus crucified you must repeat St. Ignatius' examination from the first week of the Spiritual Exercises. Ask yourselves: What have I done to crucify them? What do I do to uncrucify them? What must I do for this people to rise again?"[21]

Theologian Mary Solberg points to three forms of cruciform knowledge (what she calls "cross-oriented knowing") evoked by questions like Ellacuría's. First to emerge is a "gradual awakening, a dawning awareness, a coming to terms, a raising of consciousness."[22] This form of knowing can be likened to awakening from a nightmare that produces distress, embarrassment, even confusion. It can emerge from an experience of suffering that one cannot make sense of—whether one's own experience of suffering or that of others. The second form of cruciform knowledge entails a conversion that happens when we see and know that we are implicated and interconnected with the suffering of others. Such a conversion brings awareness of our interrelatedness—an awakening to the fact that this has happened in my world and

21. Johnson, *Quest*, 84.
22. Solberg, "All That Matters," 150.

experience, and that I am accountable for it.[23] For example, in 2018, the Trump administration mandated that immigrant children at our borders be "kidnapped" (an ironic term *Washington Post* columnist Eugene Robinson used of this practice)[24] from their parents by officers of *our* government as "punishment" for seeking a better life or asylum from violence in their home country. Some of these children were of preschool age! All of us probably have a childhood memory of the sheer terror of being separated from a parent—even if for only a moment. Thus, understandably, this horrific government-sponsored practice of separation raised difficult questions for many American Christians: Are these children really like our own, and their desperate parents really like us, trying to secure the safety and well-being of their loved ones? Are they not created in the image of God for relationship with God, others, and themselves? Answers to questions like these can bring about a conversion, enabling us to see that we are implicated in, and accountable for, the suffering of others. The third form of cruciform knowing entails empowerment for action: "The more one pays attention, sees what is the case—in Luther's wonderful phrase, 'calls the thing what it actually is'—the more one is drawn into what is going on . . . the more one feels, and then knows, oneself involved; the more one knows oneself accountable, the more one feels compelled to act with and on behalf of the neighbor(s) with whom one now stands."[25]

---

23. Solberg, "All That Matters,"151. "I am accountable for where I am, for the space I occupy. Those on the margins, those in crisis, those who suffer—drug addicts, homeless men, battered women, children with AIDS—merely by being there . . . call into question those who approach, challenging their 'being human'; and this radical questioning of what it means to be a human being serves as the historical mediation of our questioning of what 'being God' means." Solberg, "All That Matters," 152.

24. Robinson, "Does the Trump administration see Central Americans as humans?," editorial page, *Washington Post*, July 30, 2018.

25. Solberg, "All That Matters," 152–53.

Resurrection

Jesus' cross and resurrection are inseparable realities. One cannot talk about one without the other. The resurrection is the divine counteraction to violence and it discloses the God who is always and already seeking to bring life out of the death-tending ways of our world. Or as Pastor Nadia Bolz-Weber has put it, "God keeps reaching down into the dirt of humanity and resurrecting us from the graves we dig for ourselves through our violence, our lies, our selfishness, our arrogance, and our addictions. And God keeps loving us back to life over and over."[26] Our faith witnesses to the God who refuses to give up on God's good creation and who is, thus, seeking to bring life at the site of the broken places of our world. Elizabeth Johnson's perceptive image for the cross and resurrection captures these accents when she speaks of the crucified and risen Christ as the "lens" through which we interpret the living God in our midst. Through this lens "we glimpse a merciful love that knows no bounds." Jesus' life, ministry, death, and resurrection "made the love of God experientially available to all, the marginalized most of all."[27] In sum, the cross embraces both crucifixion and resurrection, for God is always at work seeking life out of wounded places.

Paul states this in another way in Galatians 2:19b–20 when he insists, "I have been crucified with Christ; and it is no longer I who live but it is Christ who lives in me." To be co-crucified and co-risen in Christ awakens and enlarges our hearts so that we are empowered to participate in the very life of God in Christ, by living in solidarity with the excluded, the vanquished, the rejected, the outsider, the profane, and the godforsaken. Co-crucifixion and co-resurrection in Christ entails radical identification with all who are crucified by abusive power and violence, and an honest confession of our own participation in all such crucifixions. In Part II of this book, we will spell out Paul's understanding of the cross and

26. Bolz-Weber, *Pastrix*, 174.
27. Johnson, *Quest*, 189–90.

resurrection as realities that create the "mystical" body of Christ in the world that resists the politics of domination and death.

This understanding of the cross and resurrection—one that entails radical identification and resistance—is poignantly expressed in Kelly Brown Douglas' powerful book *Stand Your Ground: Black Bodies and the Justice of God*. Douglas speaks about the crucified Jesus' complete identification with the Trayvon Martins of our world. As she insists, this identification "with the lynched/crucified class is not accidental. It is intentional. It did not begin with his death on the cross. In fact, that Jesus was crucified signals his prior bond with the 'crucified class' of his day."[28] Moreover, she maintains that resurrection is

> God's definitive victory over crucifying powers of evil. Ironically, the power that attempts to destroy Jesus on the cross is actually itself destroyed by the cross. The cross represents the power that denigrates human bodies, destroys life, and preys on the most vulnerable in society. As the cross is defeated, so too is that power. The impressive factor is how it is defeated. It is defeated by a life-giving rather than a life-negating force. God's power, unlike human power, is not a "master race" kind of power. That is, it is not a power that diminishes the life of another so that others might live. God's power respects the integrity of all human bodies and the sanctity of all life. This is a resurrecting power. Therefore, God's power never expresses itself through the humiliation or denigration of another. It does not triumph over life. It conquers death by resurrecting life. The force of God is a death-negating, life-affirming force.[29]

An astute member of my former church captured the cross in a striking fashion, I thought, when he observed that the horizontal bar of the cross represents the ways in which fear and violence preoccupy and oppress our lives, while the vertical bar represents the ways in which God is intersecting our death-preoccupied lives

28. Douglas, *Stand Your Ground*, 174.
29. Douglas, *Stand Your Ground*, 182.

in order to bring resurrection and life.[30] I believe that our task as Christians is to stand at those places of intersection. Dietrich Bonhoeffer, in his struggle against Nazi tyranny, put it this way: "The reality of God discloses itself only by setting me entirely in the reality of the world; but there I find the reality of the world always already created, sustained, judged, and reconciled in the reality of God."[31] In a similar vein, N. T. Wright affirms, "We humans are called to stand at the intersection of heaven and earth, holding together in our hearts, our praises, and our urgent intercessions the loving wisdom of the creator God and the terrible torments of his battered world."[32]

Summary and prayer exercise: In this chapter, I have contended that a political theology of the cross exposes sin that is both public (in our social environment) and internalized or inscribed upon us; it also awakens and directs our attention to ways in which we tend to reinscribe sin onto the world around us. A spirituality of the cross seeks to discern these inscriptions. The story about the former gang member's tattoos, and his removal of them, serves as an analogy for the marks of the crucified and risen Christ upon each of us. I have argued that the same violence that crucified Jesus crucifies us in various ways. Whether we are aware of it or not, we all bear the marks of violence upon us, perhaps not physically, but spiritually. As we look at the world through the lens of the cross, it opens our eyes to the many crucifixions happening all around us—points at which human life and God's creation suffer. Yet as the cross exposes sin, it also discloses the resurrecting power of God who is always and already bringing life out of the death-tending ways of our world.

I invite you to ponder the baptismal question cited above: do you renounce evil in the world, that which defies God's justice and love? How does evil that defies God's purposes manifest itself in crosses of racism, sexism, or classism (or other abuses of power)

30. I am grateful to Jim Spearman for this observation. Jim is an elder and key leader at The New York Avenue Presbyterian Church in Washington, DC.

31. Quoted in Ottati, *Jesus Christ*, 135.

32. Wright, *The Day*, 80.

that are inscribed upon you? Can you identify specific crosses that litter the landscape of your personal life, the life of your community, and the life of the nation? As difficult as it may be, ponder deeply how you might be caught in the web of crucifying abuses of power.

I also invite you to ponder the equally difficult questions proposed by Ignacio Ellacuría (paraphrased as follows): What have I done, or what am I doing, that crucifies others and God's good creation? Is my complicity in these crosses via sins of commission or omission? What can I do to "uncrucify" others and the creation? What can and must I do, by the Spirit of the crucified and risen Christ at work within me, to participate in God's resurrecting power for others, for myself, and for God's good creation?

Pray over these questions and your answers (both individually and in groups within your church setting), asking for God's illuminating, justice-seeking, healing, reconciling, resurrecting power to be present to you. Then take a few moments to discuss with others and write down what you have discerned.

I hope this big-picture prayer exercise with which this chapter has concluded may facilitate broad reflection on the realities of crucifixion and resurrection in our lives. The following chapter will introduce prayer exercises that facilitate more specific and focused reflection on the cross and resurrection in daily life. I hope it is becoming clear that reflection on paschal realities in our own lives is deeply intertwined with recognition of their presence in the lives of others, thereby carrying us into participation in God's work of resurrection.

2

The Cross Examen

Romans 8:11, 22–27: If the Spirit of him who raised Jesus from the dead dwells in you, he who raised Christ from the dead will give life to your mortal bodies also through his Spirit that dwells in you. . . . We know that the whole creation has been groaning in labor pains until now; and not only the creation, but we ourselves, who have the first fruits of the Spirit, groan inwardly while we wait for adoption, the redemption of our bodies. For in hope we were saved. Now hope that is seen is not hope. For who hopes for what is seen? But if we hope for what we do not see, we wait for it with patience. Likewise the Spirit helps us in our weakness; for we do not know how to pray as we ought, but that very Spirit intercedes with sighs too deep for words. And God, who searches the heart, knows what is the mind of the Spirit, because the Spirit intercedes for the saints according to the will of God. (NRSV)

Ezekiel 37:1–6: The hand of the Lord came upon me, and he brought me out by the spirit of the Lord and set me down in the middle of a valley; it was full of bones. He led me all around them; there were very many lying in the valley, and they were very dry. He said to me, "Mortal, can these bones live?" I answered, "O Lord God, you know." Then he said to me, "Prophesy to these bones, and say to them: O dry bones, hear the word of the Lord. Thus says the Lord God to these bones: I will cause breath to enter you, and you shall live. I will lay sinews on you, and will cause flesh to come upon you, and cover you with skin, and put breath in you, and you shall live; and you shall know that I am the Lord." (NRSV)

IN THIS CHAPTER WE will engage prayer exercises that facilitate discernment of the realities of crucifixion and resurrection in our daily lives and that summon and enliven our participation in God's work of bringing life out of the death-tending ways of the world. As I've reflected on the presence of the cross and resurrection in my own life and ministry, and that of my congregations, I have found myself returning often to an odd, yet inspiring, image: that of *krummholz*. *Krummholz* is the German word for twisted or crooked wood. *Krumm* means twisted and *holz* means wood. *Krummholz* trees grow on the tundra in mountainous areas where continual exposure to fierce, freezing winds stunt and deform their growth. In fact, they are like twisted bushes, so close to the ground that, from afar, you cannot always distinguish them from the tundra. I first encountered them on the slopes of Half Mountain in Colorado's Rocky Mountain National Park. At an elevation of 11,500 feet (and a six-mile round trip), one would not anticipate that the hike to the top of Half Mountain would be overly difficult; but there is no trail up the mountain and it is a relatively steep grade through dense stretches of *krummholz*. Your first inclination is to try to skirt around this stunted, sturdy, twisted vegetation, but you soon realize that this will make the hike twice as long. Thus, most hikers bushwhack right through it. Given this difficulty, you might wonder why anyone would make this hike! The answer is simple: the view at the top. There is a perch atop the mountain that provides a stunning view of the full length of Glacier Gorge, a drop-dead beautiful glacier-cut gorge that exposes majestic peaks, alpine lakes, and lush forests. The gorge is a favorite spot for wildlife. The view from Half Mountain's top is so spectacular—even dizzying—that you have to sit down. And from that perch you can watch the alpine bird life sailing upward and downward and circling about in the gorge, often below you.

The perch on Half Mountain is a powerful image for the spiritual exercises we will explore in this chapter: the Cross Examen and the Cruciform (Cross-Shaped) Breath Prayer—prayer disciplines that I have crafted utilizing the theology of the cross that we examined in chapter 1. In shaping these two prayer disciplines,

I have drawn deeply from my own experience using the Spiritual Exercises of St. Ignatius—especially the Daily Examen—and Buddhist Breath Prayer. The Cross Examen entails contemplative reflection on the movement of one's spirit upwards toward God, downwards away from God, or in circling patterns. Movements toward God can include joy, peace, love, justice, and generosity of spirit—these are movements of resurrection. Movements away from God can be occasioned by despair, depression, fear, anger, enmity, or oppression—and are movements that reflect the death-tending ways of our lives. A circling movement can feel like fatedness, dryness, or lack of movement altogether—as if your feet are trapped, your movement hindered, by dense patches of *krumm-holz*. All such movements, whether towards God or away from God, can surface in our awareness in a variety of ways: perhaps as experiences, feelings, mental images, perceptions, memories, or anticipations of the future. Now imagine that you are sitting on a perch of a mountain observing the movements of your spirit as they glide up and down and circle about, identifying each for what it is and placing it before the loving, healing, justice-seeking, and resurrecting presence of God. Imagine God as a mother holding a child in her arms—your spirit is that child, with all its movements, feelings, perceptions, or memories—all your peace, hope, despair, frustration, or anger. God is holding them as a child that is her own, a child that is perhaps crying or wounded.

I liken this practice to an experience of Good Friday, which is one reason I call it the Cross Examen. On Good Friday, one cannot help but wonder, how could the death of Jesus ever be described as "good"? How can crucifixion be good? How can despair, frustration, anger, or threatening experiences be good? We do not usually regard such experiences as beneficial! And oppressive experiences of injustice are, without question, not good. Despair is not good. Anger is not always good (although later we will consider a form of anger—"cold anger"—that could be described as good). Movement away from God is not good. When you are pressed up against, and fused within, any of these experiences, they are clearly not good, but rather suffocating and constraining. However, mindful attention to them in the safe space provided by prayer, contemplation, and mediation can provide another perspective and just enough space to recognize God as one who is with us seeking to bring transformation and liberation in the midst of these experiences. This safe space can be imagined as the perspective you gain from a perch on a mountaintop, or from an oasis in a desert. Maybe you find it sitting by a river, at a bus stop, or in a park—wherever you are able to be still long enough to observe the movements of your spirit and bring them into the presence of a loving, liberating God who seeks to bring life.

Here is another way to think of the space that allows you to observe the diverse movements of your spirit, both toward and away from God: imagine the room where the risen Christ appeared to the disciples in John's gospel (John 20:19–29). John's accounts of these resurrection appearances are notable in that the wounds of crucifixion remain on Jesus' hands and side—indeed, he not only shows the disciples his wounds, but invites Thomas to touch them. In her reflection on this story, theologian Shelly Rambo contends that the real power of the resurrection can be seen in this invitation to attend to wounds. She notes that Jesus directs the attention of his disciples toward the wounds, inviting us to do the same, with a "readiness to hold pain and to stay with difficult truths" about the wounds that remain in our own lives. Indeed, Rambo re-envisions "the meaning of resurrection . . . locating its power in confronting, not erasing, the complexities of life beyond 'deaths,' whether literal or figurative."[1] In these resurrection wounds,

> Jesus brings the memory of histories of suffering forward, and he begins to teach a way of engaging wounds. Jesus' body is marked by the social forces of his day. The crucifixion marks are signs of his denigration and humiliation. *If we follow Christian claims about the crucifixion, we can think about the crucifixion as not only the suffering of one body but also of a body that takes in the histories of suffering and bears the marks of these histories.* The claim that Jesus takes on the sins of the world can be rendered,

1. Rambo, *Resurrecting Wounds*, 150.

here, in socio-material terms. His body is marked. But
the resurrection accounts attest to a different moment,
in which the memory of that suffering returns to be engaged and the disciples are invited to receive it, to bear it.
. . . If these marks are erased, these difficult memories can
be pushed below the surface.[2]

But if wounds are brought to the surface, there is potential for
healing. Rachel Held Evans suggests as much when she speaks of
baptism as an affirmation that "God is in the business of bringing
dead things back to life . . . so if you want in on God's business, you
better prepare to follow God to all the rock-bottom, scorched earth,
dead-on-arrival corners of this world—including those in your own
heart—because . . . that's where God gardens."[3] This is certainly what
Paul is getting at, too, when he observes in Romans, "If the Spirit of
him who raised Jesus from the dead dwells in you, he who raised
Jesus from the dead will give life to your mortal bodies" (Rom 8:11).
You see, the "good" of Good Friday is perceptible when we view
our lives in light of the presence and activity of God in our lives—
the God whose primary work is seeking to bring life out of death
and resisting the death-tending realities of our world. When there
would seem to be no way out, God is already there—always present, seeking to bring life out of seemingly desperate circumstances.
This understanding of God is also grounded in the biblical notion
of God as the One who brings creation out of chaos and liberation
from enslavement. In a similar vein, the prophet Ezekiel images
God as One who speaks to exiles and brings dead, dry bones to life
with flesh, skin, and breath.

Good Friday invites us to ponder our most vulnerable experiences as places where we meet the God of resurrection and life.
This is why theologian Kristine Culp says that vulnerability is the
pivot of salvation—indeed, the point at which salvation occurs.[4]
This notion is hard to grasp because nobody wants to be vulnerable. We want to be strong and self-sufficient. But life has a way

2. Rambo, *Resurrecting Wounds*, 150 (emphasis mine).

3. Evans, *Searching for Sunday*, 21.

4. Culp, *Vulnerability and Glory*, 22.

of bearing down on us and reminding us that stand-alone self-sufficiency is an illusion. This is why we need the perch of Good Friday—a place from which we can perceive God as a mother caring for us and loving our wounded souls back to life.

I find it instructive that at the critical juncture of Paul's Letter to the Romans, the chief image for God's restoring, re-creating work is that of childbirth. The whole creation and we ourselves, says Paul, are groaning with labor pains to realize the fullness of our created nature, to be set free from bondage and be fully known as children of God (Rom 8:18–25). And the Spirit of God groans with us. Even when we do not know how to pray or what to pray for, the Spirit helps us in our weakness and intercedes for us with groans too deep for words (Rom 8:26–27). In my experience, the "perch" of deep contemplative practice is, at least initially, rarely approached with words, but often with groans and yearnings for forgiveness, liberation, love, and hope. These yearnings stem from the deep desire to be set free from the tyranny of enslaving emotional realities (e.g., anger, fear, greed, jealousy, hatred, self-hatreds, and anxiety) and oppressive circumstances that strangle our personal, spiritual, and social lives.

Groans and yearnings may be all we can utter at first, but as we discern what evokes them, it is important, eventually, to name the causes of pain and suffering, for this, too, is critical for healing and transformation. This is why philosopher Audre Lorde claims that naming the roots of pain and suffering is also critical for healing and transformation. Lorde differentiates unexamined suffering from that which is named: "Pain is an event, an experience that must be recognized, named, and then used in some way in order for the experience to change, to be transformed into something else, strength or knowledge or action."[5] Naming pain and suffering is very much akin also to the Buddhist notion of mindfulness of the roots of suffering. Zen Master Thich Nhat Hanh explains the Second Noble Truth of Buddhism in this way: "After we touch our suffering, we need to look deeply into it to see how it came to be. We need to recognize and identify the spiritual

5. Lorde, *Sister Outsider,* 89–90.

and material foods we have ingested that are causing us to suffer."[6] For me, contemplative prayer facilitates such discernment. It creates a vulnerable space in which we can observe and name the wounds that God is seeking to heal, liberate, and redeem in order to set us on a new path.

In sum, vulnerability *is* the pivot of salvation—the place where God is bringing forth life—which brings me back to *krummholz*. The twisted density of the *krummholz*, like the wood of the cross, will slow you down and maybe even at times bring you to a halt, but it also reminds you that fierce wind and tons of snow and ice in winter seasons can flatten you, but they cannot deprive you of life. The Spirit of the God who hovered over the creation at the beginning, who separated the waters of the sea so that slaves could go free, who breathed life into exiled dry bones, who time and again creates a way when there is no way, *is* the same Spirit of God in Christ who hovers over us, in every moment already at work to bring resurrection out of the death-tending ways of our lives.

The Cross Examen Exercise

Now I want to introduce you to a daily prayer exercise that I call the Cross Examen. (I strongly recommend that you engage the exercise both individually and with groups in your communal setting, for as pastoral theologian Larry Kent Graham says: "If we can share it, we can bear it."[7]) I invite you to find a place where you can experience quiet, contemplative space—a place akin to a perch on a mountaintop, an oasis in a desert, a seat by a river or at a bus stop or on a park bench, a church sanctuary or meditation room—a place of stillness from which you can observe, and identify, the movements of your life and God's life. There are three stages to the Cross Examen.

During the first stage of your prayer time, contemplate movements away from God—the "cross tending" moments in your life. Gently sift through the moments of your day (neither attaching to,

6. Hanh, *The Heart*, 9–11.

7. Graham, *Moral Injury*, 30.

or rejecting them, simply observing) when you were less than loving or when you experienced some oppressive circumstance or event in your world—experiences of movement away from God.

I call these movements (however large or small) "cross tending" because they are movements that potentially or actually mimic the same kind of power that crucified Jesus. Specifically, these movements include guilt, anxiety, anger, stresses, and fears of various sorts. To be clear, fear, anger, anxiety, and stress in and of themselves are not sin, but they have within them the potential for movement away from God, and when improperly acted upon (as we attach tightly to them), they deform and deface our lives and the lives of those around us. Such movements may come to you as feelings, mental images, perceptions, memories of the past, or anticipations of the future.

Identify or name each movement as it arises. Do not reject or attach yourself to the movement; simply observe it and place it before the loving, liberating, presence of God and allow God's resurrecting power and energy to be present to you, transforming guilt, fear, anger, anxiety, and greed into compassionate, liberating, justice-seeking love. As an aid for this first stage of contemplation, reflect with me on what "cross tending" movements away from God might look like:

Guilt: Guilt and regret are wounds of the past that can imprison us, evoked by what we have done or left undone that has marred our relationship with God and others. We are crucified by our past to the extent that we are held captive by it.

Fear: At one time or another, all of us find ourselves stuck in ditches of fear or chronic anxiety that paralyze us, deflate our sense of worth, and inhibit our actions.[8] They can shut us down, making even simple acts of compassion—of connection with others—enormously difficult. Indeed, fear and anxiety can so imprison us that we struggle with basic human ethical inclinations, such as the one Paul Ricoeur identifies with these simple words: "you too, like me."[9] They

8. Farley, *The Wounding*, 58–60.
9. Reagan, *Paul Ricoeur*, 88.

turn us in upon ourselves to such an extent that we cannot recognize our most basic interconnections with others. When others are the source of our fear, we often tend toward devaluation of them as less than ourselves (e.g., as racism, sexism, ethnocentrism, or homophobia kicks in), thereby failing to recognize our shared humanity. Whenever we do so, we mimic the same power that crucified Jesus. And when, on account of fear, we doubt our own worth, we also do violence to (or crucify) ourselves.

Anger: Sometimes anger, even rage, takes us hostage, evoked by conflicts that mar our family, work and communal environments or by the interminable warfare that marks our era. Theologian Wendy Farley observes that rage does a tricky thing to our perceptions: because our experience of harm is quite vivid, it almost always leads us to exaggerate that which was done to us, and then to magnify the inhumanity of those who harmed us. And when rage finds communal expression, it can become lethal—think of the horror of genocide throughout human history. But Farley further observes that rage does another tricky thing in addition to twisting our perceptions: it gives wounded egos another option. In contrast to the self-deflation fear produces, rage inflates one's sense of importance—"I and my cause are the only thing that counts."[10] When anger and rage are acted upon in these ways, we mimic the powers that crucified Jesus. As we will have occasion to note (chapter 7), anger and rage can be channeled in more constructive directions; e.g., anger due to experiences of injustice. The contemplative process can facilitate this transformation.

Competitiveness: Competition can evoke in us a combative sense that conquest is required. This may seem innocent enough in sports, but when it finds expression in home life, the workplace, or communal, economic, or national life, it

10. Farley, *The Wounding*, 61.

can become a deadly spiritual power that mimics that which crucified Jesus.

Greed and Jealousy: Greed and jealousy, which thrive on the sense that there is only so much of some good to go around (whether possessions, friendship, love, status, or praise), also deform us and represent movements away from God. Varied religious traditions recognize the ways in which greed and jealousy can constrain our spirits. The Buddha, for example, observed that the core of suffering "is caused when humans greedily try to break the interconnections and hold on to things just for themselves."[11] Likewise, Walter Brueggemann contends that the biblical story can be seen as a struggle between the litany of abundance and the myth of scarcity. The opening chapters of Genesis tell the story of a divine generosity and abundance so plentiful that no one can claim scarcity. But by the end of Genesis, Pharaoh appears on the scene and introduces the principle of dearth. Fearful that there is not enough, he starts greedily grabbing everything.[12] Greed, and its close cousin, jealousy, have caused great suffering throughout history, and in our consumer-driven world they have become tyrannical forces that deform and deface whole societies and the earth itself. Consumerist culture engraves upon us the message that we are "not enough": not beautiful or handsome enough, not smart enough, not rich enough. At the core of our being, we believe that we are "not enough!" Thus, at the underbelly of our culture there are devalued, deprecated, crucified selves, jealously yearning and greedily grasping for more.

Meandering: For many of us, movement away from God may be characterized not by fear or rage or competition or greed, but rather by incessant meandering without aim or purpose and frittering away of our time and energies. What are we looking for? Our lives are akin to the words we say to the

11. Knitter, *Without Buddha*, 106.
12. Brueggemann, "The Litany," 342.

salesperson in the department store: "Just looking." There is a yearning deep inside of us—to love God, others, and ourselves—that reflects the very image of God in us, yet we continue to meander, in exile from the love God intends for us. Meandering can render us passive in the face of injustices in our midst and for this reason can represent a "cross tending" movement away from God.

Egocentrism: As Wendy Farley observes, egocentrism entails an absorption with oneself due to the painful separation from love.[13] I would add that self-absorption is a kind of crucifixion in that we experience ourselves as cut off, separated, exiled from the rightly ordered loves we need.

Spiritual Violence: In chapter 1 we reflected on the spiritual violence inscribed on us and in us that represents various manifestations of crucifixion (e.g., economic injustice and classism, ethnocentrism and racism, segregation and hypersegregation, environmental degradation, sexism, heterosexism, greed, hatred, or self-hatred). In what ways have such realities deformed our lives and communities—whether we find ourselves on the giving or receiving end of them? For example, in what ways have microaggressions wounded us? In what ways have we inflicted microaggressions on others? The Korean notion of *han* is relevant here: do we bear social political, spiritual wounds due to exploitation? In what ways are such wounds inscribed on us? Jesus invites disciples to mindful attention to such wounds, for recognition of them holds the hope of healing and resurrection.

All of the above are examples of the kinds of things that might surface in your awareness as you practice contemplation. They represent movements away from God that, if acted upon inappropriately, are potentially expressions of crucifying power. Seek to discern how these or other movements away from God disfigure your life.

13. Farley, *The Wounding*, 33.

*During the second stage of your prayer time, I invite you to con-
template movements toward God—the "resurrecting" or "animating" moments in your life. Gently sift through the moments of your
day, attending to gifts of the day or your awareness of movement
toward God—gifts of joy or peace; gifts, however small, of redemption (homecoming), of liberation from oppressive circumstance, of
forgiveness and reconciliation. Give thanks and praise to God for
each gift and celebrate God's empowering, animating, transforming,
and resurrecting love.*

"Resurrection" moments may have surfaced in your awareness already during the first stage of this prayer time, as you
observed movements away from God, acknowledging them and
placing them before the loving, liberating presence of God and allowing God's resurrecting power and energy to be present to you,
transforming negative energy into compassionate, justice-seeking
love. The simple act of observation and acknowledgement of "cross
tending" movements *lessens their grip* upon us and opens up space
to recognize God's power at work within us. By attending to ways
in which both cross and resurrection find expression in our lives,
we participate in the Paschal Mystery. We are discerning the cruciform (cross-shaped) realities of our lives and celebrating God's
resurrecting power in the midst of them.

You may find it helpful to call to mind verses of Scripture
quoted at the beginning of this chapter:

> "If the Spirit of the One who raised Jesus from the dead
> dwells in you, the One who raised Jesus from the dead
> will bring life to your mortal bodies." (Romans 8:11)

> "The Spirit intercedes with sighs too deep for words."
> (Romans 8:28)

> "Thus says the LORD God to these bones: I will cause
> breath to enter you, and you shall live. I will lay sinews
> on you, and will cause flesh to come upon you, and cover
> you with skin, and put breath in you, and you shall live;
> and you shall know that I am the LORD." (Ezekiel 37:5–6)

The third stage of the Cross Examen entails a commitment to carry or bear all that we have discerned into our daily lives and the life of the world. We do so in order to create habits of mindfulness of, and participation in, the work of God's Spirit in our lives and world, bringing life out of crucifying patterns. Our lives, in other words, can conform to the image of God in Christ—to the pattern of the crucified and resurrected Christ—for as Paul says, we are "always carrying in the body the death of Jesus, so that the life of Jesus may also be made visible in our bodies" (2 Cor 4:10). This commitment entails "seeing" the world differently, with the prophetic vision that stems from bearing the cross. In his book *The Prophets*, Rabbi Abraham Joshua Heschel describes the prophet as one who is "thrown into" the world and is scandalized by what she or he sees. Heschel draws a stark contrast between ordinary sight and prophetic vision: "To us a single act of injustice—cheating in business, exploitation of the poor—is slight; to the prophet, a disaster. To us injustice is injurious to the welfare of the people; to the prophet it is a deathblow to existence; to us, an episode; to them, a catastrophe, a threat to the world."[14] Moreover, the prophetic vision of cross bearing facilitates deep connection of our own brokenness with that of others. As Thich Nhat Hanh observes, "Our happiness and suffering are the happiness and suffering of others. . . . When we look at others we see how their happiness and suffering are linked to our happiness and suffering."[15] *In sum, the commitment to bearing the cross and resurrection entailed in the third stage of this exercise gives birth to engaged spirituality—a commitment to see our common life differently and to participate in places where God is bringing life out of the death-tending ways of our world.*

I encourage you to spend ten to thirty minutes a day in the Cross Examen, at whatever time of day is good for you. And at the end of each prayer period, note in a journal your experiences of the movements of your life and of God's Spirit at work in the midst of them. What happened in the prayer time? Did you experience energy—God's resurrecting power? You do not need to do more

14. Heschel, *The Prophets*, 4.
15. Hanh, *The Heart*, 148–49.

than sketch what you experienced. If you do this on a regular basis, the written accounts of your prayer experience can become an aid in discerning how God is at work in your life, healing or liberating you, or where God is calling you.

The Cruciform (Cross-Shaped) Breath Prayer

Here is a second prayer exercise that I also commend to you: the Cruciform (Cross-Shaped) Breath Prayer—the simplest prayer that I know. I find myself praying in this way both at designated times and at random, stressful moments of the day (sometimes in a meeting, at a traffic light, or while waiting in line). It captures, in summary form, the essence of the Cross Examen explicated above. You do not need to choose between the two. They are simply two modes of praying, both of which attend to the Paschal Mystery—that is, to the realities of crucifixion and resurrection in our lives. You may benefit from both. (I recommend, again, that you engage this exercise individually and with groups within your communal setting.)

Here is the *Cruciform (Cross-Shaped) Breath Prayer*, which can be used at any time and place—all that is required is awareness of your breath:

Breathe in. As you do so, sense the resurrecting, forgiving, compassionate, justice-seeking power of God's Spirit filling you with energy.

Exhale. As you breathe out, mindfully name (neither attaching to, or rejecting—simply observing) and let go of the disfiguring, toxic realities that deform your relationship with God, others, and yourself. For example, breathe out the potentially crucifying effects of any guilt, fear, insecurity, anxiety, or anger.[16] Let

16. As noted above, anxiety, fear, and anger are not, in and of themselves, sin (or crucifiers), but when we fuse to them and improperly act upon them, they can become sin (or contribute to crucifixion—to acts, large or small, that mimic the same power that crucified Jesus). To be crucified with Christ (Gal 2:19–20, 6:14) is to be liberated from potentially deforming, tyrannical enmities that breed fear, insecurity, and anger within oneself or toward God and others.

go of greed or jealousy. Release spiritual violations that have come your way through expressions of racism, sexism, classism, or homophobia. Allow God's resurrecting Spirit to transform the potential crucifying effects of guilt, fear, insecurity, anxiety, or anger into compassionate, forgiving, and justice-seeking love.

Sense the luminosity of the image of God in Christ as you breathe in God's life-giving Spirit and breathe out all of those things that deform your relationships with God, others, and yourself.

Seek to stay with this awareness as you breathe throughout your day, conscious of your interconnection[17] with God, every-one, and everything. Compassionately and nonviolently resist all that deforms others and yourself. Live into God's transform-ing presence.

The Cross Examen takes the cross as its point of departure; the Breath Prayer starts with the power of resurrection. Though I have described a sequential process for both exercises, the steps in each could be reversed, for the movement between cross and resurrection is fluid and cyclical. Wherever crosses litter the land-scape of our lives, there also is the resurrecting power of God; and wherever there are signs of resurrection, there also are the wounds of the cross. The two are deeply intertwined in our individual and corporate lives. Thus, you can start with reflection on resurrection or conclude with it, for Christians are post-resurrection people, which is to say that resurrection is the pervasive reality of God in Christ in which we live in every moment of our lives—embraced by a love that will not let us go. The hope and promise of both the Cross Examen and the Cruciform (Cross-Shaped) Breath Prayer is that the God who raised Jesus from the dead can transform our fears and anxieties into liberation, courage, and action; our rage and anger into compassionate justice-seeking; and our obsessions, addictions, and self-absorptions into loving, relational community. Transformation, of course, is rarely instantaneous—it takes time

17. Interconnection means that what crucifies one, crucifies all; and what liberates one, liberates all.

and involves both personal and communal practice in a setting where love, compassion, trust, and accountability are shared values—values rooted in the Spirit of the crucified and risen Christ. In the Appendix to this book, I offer an example from my own ministry of how the Cross Examen and Cruciform Breath Prayer can be used in a communal setting.

Part II

Cruciform Spirituality and Political Practice

A New Perspective on Galatians

NEW TESTAMENT SCHOLAR BRIGITTE Kahl's brilliant reimagining of Paul's letter to the churches in the Roman province of Galatia provides an interpretive springboard for fresh reflection on what engaged or cruciform spirituality might mean for us today—a spirituality of the cross that reveals the broken places in our lives and in the life of the world where God's resurrection power is at work bringing life out of death. Biblical texts are, to be sure, multivalent—which is to say that they bear a range of meanings. No single interpretation can ever fully capture these deeply generative texts, but new readings can deepen and broaden our engagement with them. Brigitte Kahl's innovative reading of Galatians is a case in point. In Part II of this book, we will engage her compelling interpretation as a foundation for reflection on spiritual, social, and political dimensions of this ancient Pauline letter. First, we will consider Kahl's interpretation of Galatians; then we will explore the fruit of the Spirit in Galatians 5:22–23 as political virtues for cruciform faith and action.

3

Galatians and Cruciform Spirituality

AN ARRESTING SCULPTURE COMMONLY known as "The Dying Gaul," also called "The Dying Galatian," is housed in the Capitoline Museum in Rome. It portrays a wounded Galatian warrior crumpled on his shield and defenseless. The warrior's sword and shattered trumpet lie on the ground, both sure signs of defeat. The combatant's muscular body is naked and vulnerable. The sculpture is thought to be of the same kind and intent as the Great Altar of Pergamum in the Roman province of Galatia—a sculptural project that dates between 180 and 160 BCE. The altar and the sculpture functioned as Roman propaganda, as they depicted Rome's defeat of the Gallic menace in the most dramatic terms. The Gauls are pictured as barbaric, lawless, and demonic—a presentation that aimed to justify Roman violence against them.

Both the Dying Gaul and the Great Altar of Pergamum feature prominently in Brigitte Kahl's compelling book on Paul's letter to the churches of Galatia, *Galatians Re-Imagined: Reading with the Eyes of the Vanquished*. Kahl claims that when Galatians is read in the context of Roman imperial religion (represented by statues like the Dying Gaul and the Great Altar of Pergamum), the main target of Paul's fury in the letter is not Judaism, as interpreters have long assumed, but rather imperial religion—a religion that justifies violence to subjugate people and that ensures right relationship with Caesar, the god of Roman law and religion. Consider Kahl's description of the statue of the Dying Gaul and the message it conveyed:

> Sitting on the ground, the Gaul has his one arm propped up in a position between rising once again and final collapse. The same contradictory impulses are embodied in his feet. The left is still up; with his leg forming an arch over the broken horn underneath, the right has already collapsed.... This man is still sufficiently alive to be truly menacing and to showcase the fortitude of his victor, but he is too injured to pose any realistic threat.... Yet it is this very moment of dying, frozen in timelessness, that has made him immortal, encapsulating a message that was as vital for ... Romans as for their Western imperial successors.... It is a message about sacred violence and the basic order of the world, about victory and civilization: our civilization.[1]

In other words, the statue celebrates Roman subjugation of barbarian and lawless peoples (for the Gauls/Galatians were the chief historical enemies of Rome). All who publicly acknowledge the divine necessity of this subjugation are brought into right relationship with the God of Roman law and imperial religion. Eerily, Kahl's description of the Dying Gaul is similar to theologian Kelly

1. Kahl, *Galatians Re-Imagined*, 77–78.

Brown Douglas's haunting depiction of the black body in American racial history and contemporary culture:

> The very construction of the black body as an uncontrollable beast, given its hypersexualized nature, means this body must be controlled. Indeed, as natural law theo-ideology contends, control of this body is for the common good. A free black body is tantamount to a wild animal on the loose. So, once again, a free black body is, according to the productions of America's exceptionalist narrative, quintessentially a dangerous black body.[2]

The resonance is uncanny: though separated by 2,000 years, the symbolism is the same. Gauls and blacks are viewed by their respective dominant (racist) cultures as savage, requiring violence to control them.

The same ideology of domination was present in the Great Altar of Pergamum, which depicted a decisive battle in which the Gauls were defeated. This altar, according to Kahl, was a kind of megachurch for the celebration of imperial religion within the Galatian territories, and a not-so-subtle reminder that Caesar was Lord of all.[3] The Altar would have been well known to the churches of Galatia, and their neighbors would have noticed whether or not church members were participating in the megachurch celebrations. (In like manner, minoritized athletes who do not stand for the National Anthem have been noticed, and reviled, as insufficiently patriotic, in our own cultural context.)

Those with even slight acquaintance with Paul's letter to the Galatians may find themselves wondering, as did I, when I first read Kahl's book: What about circumcision—the most prominent issue in the letter? Galatians is in many respects a single-issue letter, for in it Paul strongly objects to the fact that male Gentile believers are being lured into the practice of circumcision. In the long history of interpretation, commentators have assumed that Paul is addressing a Jewish-Christian perversion of the gospel that promoted works righteousness. But when one

2. Douglas, *Stand Your Ground*, 70.
3. Douglas, *Stand Your Ground*, 166.

takes the Roman imperial context into account, this aspect of Paul's letter looks quite different. You see, Roman law did not require Jews to participate fully in the imperial cult. Jews were granted an exception—a back door of respectability that did not require of them full recognition of Caesar's divinity. They had to pray on behalf of the emperor and offer sacrifices on his behalf, but they were otherwise exempt from worship in the megachurch of imperial Rome. They were a special case.

Take this into account as you consider the serious bind in which Gentile Christians, and Galatian Gentile Christians at that, found themselves. First of all, the fact that your people (the Gauls/Galatians) were historic enemies of Rome was enshrined in public media—in statues such as the Dying Gaul and the Great Altar of Pergamum. Therefore, if you did not believe in Caesar's lordship and refused to join in the practice of imperial religion, people would surely notice and you might find yourself under suspicion of insurrection. Second, if you confessed the lordship of Jesus, who was crucified as a rebel against Rome—one who was raised from the dead and now Lord of all—you found yourself in a double bind, and a politically incendiary bind at that! In short, if you were a Galatian Gentile Christian, you might perceive that you had two choices: either abandon your faith in Jesus as Lord and reinstate your membership in Rome's megachurch or, under the disguise of Torah, become a circumscribed Jew and take the back door to respectability.[4] In short, you could "pass" as a Jew, thereby avoiding participation in the imperial cult. The latter, according to Kahl, is what Galatian Christians were opting for. They were mightily tempted, for very good reasons, to try to "pass" as Jews. But there was a catch to this option that provoked Paul's ire: *under the guise of Torah*, they were allowing age-old divisions and enmities between Jews and Gentiles to remain unreconciled in the community of the crucified and resurrected Christ. In other words, the union in Christ of Jews as Jews and Gentiles as Gentiles, Paul's vision for the church as a beachhead of new creation, was being nullified. *Moreover, they also were re-inscribing*

4. Kahl, *Galatians Re-Imagined*, 219–27.

the domination system of the empire.[5] Indeed, they were allowing the very system that crucified Christ to stay in place, unchecked and unchallenged by the countercultural witness of a community in which racial, gender, and economic justice and reconciliation were embodied under the lordship of Christ.

What strikes me about the Galatian problem is the way in which it reflects a perennial danger of Christian faith: co-optation by the powers that be, with the result that the church can end up supporting the status quo, allowing the faith to be governed by something other than the gospel. This is the same aspect of the human condition we noted in the introduction to this volume: the perennial danger of being co-opted, hijacked, gerrymandered, or, to use biblical imagery, exiled and enslaved, by "not gods" (Gal 4:8) that warp and crucify us. To put it succinctly, this was the problem with the Galatian church as Paul saw it—the co-optation of the gospel. Gentile Christians, by accepting circumcision and "passing" as Jews, were able to live their lives without threat of persecution and unburdened by Emperor worship; but they were also giving Caesar a "pass": his rule was unobstructed, because they were accommodating, rather than resisting, imperial ways. A monochrome community of Jewish-Christians was hardly the beachhead of "new creation" that Paul envisioned for the church. It was hardly a community of mutuality that embodied justice amid prevailing hierarchies of race, ethnicity, gender, and economic status (Gal 3:28). The Galatian churches, through their failure to bear public witness to the faith as an alternative community united under a different lordship, were allowing hierarchies of domination to go unchecked. They were co-opted by Caesar and his rule. And to make matters worse, they were doing it in the name of Torah—in the name of religion—with the result that the radically monotheistic Torah itself was being hijacked by Caesar.

Sadly, co-optation by the powers that be is a temptation the church faces in every age. Indeed, it continues to subvert the church's public witness to the gospel of a crucified and risen Lord in our own time and place. Sobering recent examples readily present

5. Kahl, "Galatians," 512 (emphasis mine).

themselves. In the 2016 US presidential election, for instance, a whopping 85 percent of evangelical Christians helped elect a candidate who ran on a platform that was explicitly anti-Muslim, anti-immigrant, homophobic, sexist, and racist. Was this not a tragic betrayal of the gospel of Jesus Christ to which Scripture bears witness? An instance in which the gospel of a crucified and risen Lord was co-opted by agendas other than reconciling, justice-seeking love? Moreover, an alarming rising tide of Neo-Nazi and KKK associations in this country, which spews hatred towards Jews, Muslims, and gays, often does so explicitly in the name of Christianity. Is this not also a betrayal—indeed, an astounding perversion—of the gospel? There are of course many more subtle ways in which Christians are co-opted by powers that be and fail to bear public witness to their faith, often through silence and passivity—by not speaking out and not taking a stand against practices such as racial profiling by law enforcement officers, housing policies that reflect racial bias, the deporting of thousands of law-abiding, hard-working, yet undocumented immigrants, the banning and stigmatizing of Muslims, and economic policies that marginalize whole groups of people. Countless other betrayals of the gospel could be noted, and they all reflect a similar crisis addressed in Paul's letter to the churches of Galatia. It is no wonder the apostle was so angry!

Indeed, for Paul, the back-door approach to respectability that Galatians were opting for represented going back to business as usual—as if nothing had changed, when in fact the death and resurrection of Jesus had changed everything. How could those who believed in the lordship of Jesus Christ accommodate imperial megachurch religion, wherein right relation with God in Caesar was established via violence and subordination? Were they not to live in this world as a beachhead of God's new creation—a new community united under Christ's lordship in which there was no longer Jew or Greek (alienating divisions and subordinations based in religion and race), no longer slave or free (alienating divisions and subordinations based in class and economics), and no longer male and female (alienating divisions and subordinations based in gender)? As Paul insists in Galatians 2:19–20, "I have been crucified with Christ; and it is no longer I who live, but Christ who lives in me." To be co-crucified and co-risen in Christ is not only to live in union with the excluded, the vanquished, the profane, and the godforsaken; it is also is to exclude oneself from the realm of privilege, for it entails radical identification with all who are crucified by power and violence, and a radical confession of our own participation in all such crucifixions.

Just as important, to be crucified with Christ and co-risen in Christ is to live as if death and its surrogates have no power over us. It entails radical love of God and neighbor. Thus, to be co-risen with Christ is to live free from obsessive *competitive advantage* that sees others as a threat to our well-being; free from *fear that paralyzes* us into collaboration with injustice; free from *greed that over-consumes* the goods of the earth entrusted to our care; and free from *hatreds and self-hatreds* that constrict our minds and hearts and obstruct true love of others and ourselves. To be co-crucified and co-risen in Christ is what Brigitte Kahl calls the new creation—a new community of love and mutuality through the "birth canal" of the cross and resurrection whereby we are re-made in the image of God, and become one with others rather than consumers of others.[6]

In short, Paul's vision for the Galatians and for us entails the demolition of division and enmity, and the existence in this world of a new community that reflects this demolition—a community that embraces, rather than eliminates, human diversity, thereby embodying the vision of Galatians 3:28. By trying to "pass" as Jews, Gentile Galatians threatened the integrity of their witness as a beachhead of the new creation. This new creation is made possible by our union with the crucified and risen Christ.

Paul's grand vision of the choice facing followers of Jesus Christ in every time and place echoes the book of Deuteronomy, in which Moses sets a stark choice before the ancient Israelites before their entrance into the promised land: "I have set before you life and death, blessings and curses. Choose life" (Deut 30:19). The gist of Paul's version of Deuteronomy is captured in the crucifixion

6. Kahl, *Galatians Re-Imagined*, 289.

43

and resurrection of Jesus. *Death* is that which mimics the power that crucified Jesus, and one never has to look far to discern its presence. In our day, for example, the politics of death reigns in the growing gulf between the haves and the have nots, mass incarceration and racialized police violence, joblessness or the absence of good paying jobs, nativism and the demonization of immigrants, politics that is bought and sold to the highest bidder, and obsessive glorification of the good life of mass consumption. *Life*, by contrast, is living in the same Spirit of God that raised Jesus from the dead. It is what Brigitte Kahl calls "the politics of love" defined as "the new human being and a truly humane order" that involves a "revolutionary movement from self to other" wherein "the ego loses and retrieves itself in the other, for the other, through the other, with the other, constantly dying and being resurrected, living no longer as self but as the mystical body of Christ."[7]

So when Paul speaks of "works of the flesh" and "fruit of the Spirit" in Galatians 5, contrasting vices and virtues, he has the vision of Deuteronomy and crucifixion and resurrection in mind. The works of the flesh are those that mimic crucifixion: things such as idolatry, strife, jealousy, anger, quarrels, dissension, factions, and envy. The fruit of the Spirit are empowered by co-crucifixion and co-resurrection with Christ: love, peace, joy, patience, kindness, generosity, faithfulness, gentleness, and self-control. And while these lists may strike us as a random laundry list of vices and virtues, they are, for Paul, refracted through the cross and resurrection. He insists that those who belong to Christ have crucified the flesh and its vices in order to live by the Spirit—the same Spirit that raised Jesus from the dead. Paul's vision was to create communities founded in the politics of love that could resist the politics of death.

In short, when Paul contrasts works of the flesh and fruit of the Spirit, he is talking about life trajectories that are either death-tending or life-giving. The manner in which he contrasts them clearly conveys a pitched battle between the two. In Paul's day, the battleground was laid out and the choice was clear. Would the Galatians

7. Kahl, *Galatians Re-Imagined*, 269.

opt for Caesar and his way in the world—that is, for continuing imperial domination of the Gauls? Could they dare to engage in iconoclastic worship of a Jewish rebel whom Caesar crucified—one acknowledged as Lord of all, whose resurrected life and Spirit embodied a divine power radically different from Rome's?

These questions are profoundly relevant for us today, for imperial reality is still with us. What is the nature of empire today? What do imperial realities look like and how do they affect our lives? How are Christians to respond to powers that deform and deface human life and creation? Are the fruit of the Spirit political virtues, as well as individual ones—public virtues of nonviolent, relational, and resistant love? Kahl does not elaborate on Paul's discussion of the fruit of the Spirit in Galatians 5, but her reimagining of Galatians provides rich food for thought and exploration of them. In the next nine chapters, we will reflect on the fruit of the Spirit, focusing on how each one and its collective manifestation constitute political virtues for engaged or cruciform spirituality.

The Fruit of the Spirit as Political Virtues

> Live by the Spirit, I say, and do not gratify the desires of the flesh. . . . [T]he fruit of the Spirit is love, joy, peace, patience, kindness, generosity, faithfulness, gentleness, and self-control. There is no law against such things. And those who belong to Christ Jesus have crucified the flesh with its passions and desires. (Gal 5:16, 22–24)

PAUL'S DISCUSSION OF THE "fruit of the Spirit" in Galatians 5 is among the most memorable and well-loved passages in the letter. But reflection on the significance of the virtues it represents is often narrowly confined to individual, interpersonal realms. However, as we have noted, the cross of Jesus Christ was a manifestly public event with decidedly communal and political implications for all who are baptized into Christ's death and resurrection. In the chapters that follow, building on Kahl's reimagining of Galatians, we will consider each fruit of the Spirit, exploring how its collective manifestation constitutes a political virtue for engaged cruciform spirituality—desperately needed virtues in a violent, polarized world.

But first, a few words of introduction are in order about the chapter in which Paul's catalogue of fruit of the Spirit appears. After four chapters of intense polemics, Galatians 5 marks the point at which Paul begins to draw his conclusion in a positive way, summoning the Galatians to live into the freedom from bondage that is the liberating gift of God in Jesus Christ. The keynote is sounded in 5:1: "For freedom Christ has set us free. Stand firm, therefore, and do not submit again to a yoke of slavery." Believers are given to understand that they have been set free from whatever binds them to live in the sphere of Christ's lordship, set free to live in service of God, and thus set free to serve one another in love, for love is the proper exercise of freedom. Freedom, in other words, as commentator Sam Williams insightfully summarizes it, "is not a good in itself. It is rather a means to the great good of human relationship. Freedom is not untrammeled personal autonomy. It is, rather, opportunity and possibility—the opportunity to love the neighbor without hindrance, the possibility of creating human communities based on mutual self-giving rather than the quest for power and status."[1] Such freedom is not a "possession" but a reality into which we are to live; else we can find ourselves in bondage to former masters.

Paul further establishes in Galatians 5 that the Christian life of freedom and love is not accomplished by the strength of our own wills or efforts; it is rather guided and made possible by God's own Spirit—an eschatological gift of power. Thus, Paul exhorts believers to "live" or (even better) to "*walk* by the Spirit" (5:16)—to rely on the power of God available to them, thereby leaning into God's future as it struggles toward realization now. What might that look like? In 5:16–26, Paul provides a vivid illustration of the alternatives before us with a catalogue of virtues and vices that contrasts the "works of the flesh" and the "fruit of the Spirit." Paul is confident that those who walk by the Spirit, relying on the power of God available to them, will not gratify the desires of the flesh (5:16). But an important point of clarification is needed as we approach this catalogue, for Paul's understanding of "flesh" and "Spirit" is frequently misunderstood. "Flesh" is not a reference to the body or sexuality. (Modern translations do not help us when they render the Greek word *sarx* as "lower nature" [NEB, Phillips], "sinful nature" [NLT], or "physical desires" [GNT]). And "Spirit" is not a reference to something nonmaterial and otherworldly, a reference to our "higher nature." Note well:

---

1. Williams, *Galatians*, 145.

to Paul's way of thinking, "flesh" and "Spirit" do not designate two parts of human nature but rather represent two
ways of living. Both "flesh" and "Spirit" are ways of char-
acterizing the *whole* self in relation to God. "Flesh," on the
one hand, describes human nature as a whole when it is
dominated by sin and thus has broken away from God. It
denotes a self-centered existence, in which the entire perspective of human beings is turned in upon themselves, so
that the self becomes the center of all values.[2]

(The new Contemporary English Bible translation captures this
distinction in its rendering of 5:16: "I say be guided by the Spirit
and you won't carry out your selfish desires.") Life in the "Spirit,"
on the other hand, is life set free from such bondage. Paul speaks
here not of a human spirit, but of God's Spirit—God's eschatological gift of power. "Flesh" and "Spirit," then, are each "domains of
power, spheres of influence in which one lives."[3] Indeed, human
creatures are caught in a tug of war between the two (5:17). Paul
starkly contrasts the destructive, death-tending "works of the
flesh" (5:19-21) with the life-giving "fruit of the Spirit" (5:22-23),
hoping that believers will be persuaded to entrust themselves to
the power of God, for "those who belong to Jesus Christ," who
have shared in his death in baptism, have been empowered to embrace a new way of life. Indeed, they "have crucified the flesh with
its passions and desires" (5:24).

Finally, for our purposes, it is especially important to note
that the catalogue of the "works of the flesh" and the "fruit of the
Spirit" (5:19-23) highlights the fact that Christian existence is essentially corporate in character, for the "works of the flesh" and the
"fruit of the Spirit" are detailed in largely communal categories.[4]
The catalogue of "works of the flesh" includes a central list that
details offenses against community: "enmities, strife, jealousy, anger, quarrels, dissensions, factions, envy" (5:19-21). These are sins

2. Gench, "Galatians 5:1, 13-26," 293-94.

3. Gench, "Galatians 5:1, 13-26," 294.

4. Gench, "Galatians 5:1, 13-26," 294. I am indebted to Frances Taylor
Gench for exegetical insights conveyed in this introduction.

against community, for the self-centered orientation of the "flesh" manifests itself in ways that are destructive of it. The catalogue of the "fruit of the Spirit," as we will see, is also social in nature, enumerating graces that nurture and build up community. Paul gives us to understand that these graces do not represent human accomplishments, for they are pointedly described not as "works" but rather as "fruit"—as the result of the transforming power of God's own Spirit. They are manifestations of the gift of God in human lives and communities and, as will see, they have decidedly public implications. Their collective manifestations constitute political virtues for engaged, cruciform spirituality.

4

Love: The Foundational Fruit of the Spirit

THE FRUIT OF THE Spirit in Galatians 5 is not presented as a random catalogue of virtues. It is important to note that when Paul speaks of such fruit, love heads the list. It has pride of place as the foundational fruit of the Spirit, the chief Christian virtue. Indeed, as Victor Paul Furnish has observed, "This list may be regarded as a description of the concrete ways in which love is expressed."[1] In our own cultural context, we tend to think of love as an emotion, and thus may need to be reminded that love, in the biblical idiom, is not so much something you *feel*, but rather something you *do*. It is an action rather than a feeling—an action on behalf of another's well-being—sometimes regardless of how we feel. And what might that look like?

I caught a clear glimpse of it in a Chicago neighborhood featured on the PBS Newshour in December 2016. The year 2016 was the deadliest on the streets of Chicago in more than two decades—500 homicides, ninety in August alone. Yet on a street corner in Englewood, one of the hardest hit streets on the city's South Side where several men, a woman, and a child had been killed in years past, something changed. In what was once a war zone, a grill was fired up, people gathered with lawn chairs, kids were playing—it looked like a party was going on. What happened? According to Tamar Manasseh, founder of Mothers Against Senseless Killings, "We just showed up. That's all we have

---

1. Furnish, *Theology and Ethics in Paul*, 88.

to do. Show up, grab a lawn chair and a pair of sunglasses, and you can do this. You can change the world with that." Ever since Tamar and others began showing up, there has not been a single shooting in this neighborhood.[2] There is more to showing up, of course, than is apparent at first glance: showing up is connecting deeply to vulnerable people in a neighborhood where folk would otherwise be prisoners in their own homes. But whatever shape it takes, love has a lot to do with showing up.

This was further impressed upon me when a group within my former congregation (The New York Avenue Presbyterian Church in Washington, DC) made a collective commitment to show up every other Tuesday morning during 2016 and 2017 for a particular gathering that generated deep connections. For lack of a better name, we called it the "Jobs Club." Doug, a deacon who oversees NYAPC's Radcliffe Room Homeless Program, spread the word among homeless friends who were looking for a job, inviting them to come and talk. When we gathered for conversation, we reflected together with them on job skills, work history, where they might find work or a stable environment where they could sleep and eat—so that they would be fresh for an interview and a job. Various members of NYAPC contributed to this initiative. David helped those in search of employment think about their skill sets and work up resumes. Phil, an activist lawyer, consulted with them on legal issues. Tyler, a technology whiz, facilitated Internet information and access. My colleague, associate pastor Alice, and I added whatever we could. But more than anything else we were connecting with John, Russell, José, Johnny, and a woman with a wonderful name, Fynale (pronounced "Finally"), who was teaching other homeless women how to make jewelry. In some cases there were results: one man started a lawn care business, another got a job with a concrete company, and yet another landed a job with a window contractor. And it happened simply because we were all showing up. After our initial meetings, we asked our homeless friends whether this was worth doing, and

2. *PBS Newshour,* "After Another Bloody Weekend in Chicago," December 26, 2016.

one man said enthusiastically, "Yes, coming here to talk about work and get encouragement, if not ideas, for jobs is helpful!" The commitment to showing up facilitated deep connections with folk who would otherwise be isolated and overlooked, with the odds stacked against them—not just because they are homeless, but in some cases because they also had criminal records that made work difficult to find. So just like the Mothers Against Senseless Killing who are trying to take back their neighborhood in Chicago, our homeless friends, too, will have to fight the system, and we hope we can accompany and support them in so doing.

The deep connections being made eventually bore more fruit. In fact, at the end of 2017, several members of The New York Avenue Presbyterian Church (including participants in the Jobs Club and the Radcliffe Room ministry) began a conversation with the Downtown Business Improvement District and the Washington, DC Department of Human Services to think strategically about establishing a downtown homeless center housed at the church that would provide a comprehensive array of services in one location—inclusive of employment and housing assistance, mental and physical health services, and access to food, computers, showers, and laundry facilities. In 2019, the Downtown Day Services Center became a reality. Now it serves about 160 homeless people a day—a facility that never would have materialized if a dedicated group had not committed to showing up and connecting with our homeless friends.

I believe this is, in essence, what Paul was urging the churches he founded within the Roman province of Galatia to do: to show up and embody an alternative witness; indeed, to create cells of relational resistance and transformation that deconstructed prevailing social divisions. The odds, to be sure, were stacked against believers in Galatian churches if they aspired to be anything other than conquered, defeated people. Indeed, as noted in chapter 3, if you place the politics of the Roman Empire in the foreground of Paul's letter to these churches, what emerges is a social and political milieu that aimed to integrate subjugated people into the Roman colonial mentality. Inscriptions of domination that reinforced social hierarchy were part of the air that people breathed—in statuary, legal practices, the imperial cult, and even Rome's savage entertainment industry, which featured staged games in which gladiators, usually slaves or captives, fought to the death with other gladiators, wild animals, or condemned criminals. This was all part of Roman imperial religion and is what Paul refers to pointedly as "another gospel" to which he objects in Galatians 1:6.

It was in this kind of world, a hierarchical culture of conquest and domination, that Paul made a stunning statement: a baptismal affirmation that "there is neither Jew nor Gentile, neither slave nor free, nor is there male and female, for you are all one in Christ Jesus" (Gal 3:28). This affirmation was revolutionary, turning the world upside down, which seems to have been Paul's intent. As Brigitte Kahl puts it, for Paul, the entire imperial model of "divide and rule" was drowned and washed away in the waters of baptism. The distinctive markers that created binary oppositions of "us and them" were washed away.[3] In Paul's view, if we have caught a glimpse of God's character in the crucified and risen Christ, then we are compelled to create communities that manifest the new creation, in which all such distinctions are overcome and transformed. This is "a 'revolutionary' movement of self to other" in which one loses an abusive perception of oneself in order to retrieve oneself "in the other, for the other, through the other, with the other, constantly dying and being resurrected, living no longer as the old self but as the mystical body of Christ" in baptism.[4] For Paul the opposition of "us versus them" is drowned, washed away in baptism. The result is a community of "we" or "us" in which cutthroat competition is dissolved. This, in visible communal and political terms, is what love looks like and is integral to the church's public witness in the world.

In sum, when Paul speaks of "works of the flesh" and "fruit of the Spirit" in Galatians 5, he is contrasting vices and virtues that are not only individual, but also public and political. Indeed, Paul's strategic vision was to create communities founded in the

3. Kahl, "Galatians," 515–16.
4. Kahl, *Galatians Re-Imagined*, 269.

politics of love that could resist the politics of death—communities in which fruit of the Spirit are embodied in ways visible enough to challenge the world. As he insists, "those who belong to Christ Jesus have crucified the flesh with its passions and desires. If we live by the Spirit, let us also be guided by the Spirit. Let us not become conceited, competing against one another, envying one another" (Gal 5:24–26). When Paul speaks of the fruit of the Spirit it is critical to remember that he is speaking of the same Spirit who raised Jesus from the dead, for that same Spirit is working resurrection life in us.

Moreover, *love*, the foundational fruit of the Spirit, is always cruciform, which is to say that it is cross-shaped and entails the "revolutionary" movement of self to other. One *loves* by letting go of a false sense of oneself in order to retrieve an infinitely more robust self in relation to others. To be co-crucified and co-risen in Christ is to participate in what Brigitte Kahl calls the new creation—a new community of love and mutuality through the "birth canal" of the cross and resurrection, whereby we are remade in the image of God, and become one with others rather than consumers of others.[5] The politics of death, for Paul, must be resisted.

Resisting the politics of death can come with a cost. Those who do so can find themselves excoriated as insufficiently patriotic, even treasonous. Lest there be any doubt about this, consider former NFL football players Colin Kaepernick and Eric Reid. When they took a knee during the National Anthem before a game in 2016, in order to protest police brutality and racialized violence, and inspired other NFL players to do the same, they were widely reviled as unpatriotic, even by the president of the United States. In the years since, Kaepernick has continued to be censured for his protest, denied the opportunity to resume playing in the NFL. A little-known fact is that Kaepernick and Reid are devout Christians who saw themselves as witnessing to their faith.[6] In so doing, they were following in the tradition of Martin Luther King Jr., the black

5. Kahl, *Galatians Re-Imagined*, 289.

6. Kuruvilla, "Here's What," www.huffingtonpost.com; Reid, "Why Colin Kaepernick," www.nytimes.com.

church, and other Christians during the civil rights movement who called on this nation to live up to its ideals.

This is, I think, the kind of witness and resistance that Paul had in mind for the Galatian churches, for he, too, had a respect for good government that did not arrogate divinity to itself and use violence to subjugate its people. In Romans 13, Paul contends that good government serves God's purpose when it pursues justice and restrains evil for all of its citizens, and in so doing checks tyranny. Caesar is not mentioned in Romans 13, but he is, to be sure, a target of this discourse. At the very least, Romans 13 represents a demotion for Caesar, for some Roman emperors welcomed proclamation as a god. Paul makes it very clear that governing authorities are subject to God and are not themselves gods! We can be equally sure that the church, in Paul's view, was to embody a counter-witness to tyranny and violence. The church, in other words, in Paul's day and ours, is called to "take a knee," to show up, to take to the streets in embodied witness to cruciform love.

The Roman mentality is still part of the air we breathe, reflected ad nauseum in rhetoric about "winners" and "losers." Losers are those who have failed, who have been beaten to death, if not physically, then spiritually; and winners continue to inscribe domination upon them. To be great is to win, to vanquish one's foes. But if we can embrace Paul's vision in his letter to the churches of Galatia, it can inspire us to embody God's gift of a new community of love and mutuality through the "birth canal" of the cross and resurrection, whereby we become one with others rather than abusers of others.

You may recall that the Occupy Wall Street movement that began in September 2011 sometimes entailed protests in front of churches—not because the young people in that secular sociopolitical movement were protesting what the church claimed to believe. What they were actually saying was, "Church, act like the church!" And to act like the church is to visibly embody love, the foundational fruit of the Spirit—and if I understand what that means, it has a lot to do with "showing up." In so doing, we may lose false and destructive selves and retrieve more robust selves in relationships with others, especially with the most vulnerable in our midst—the homeless, the immigrant, the refugee, the residents of violent neighborhoods. The Spirit that raised Jesus from the dead summons us to just such places and to just such persons and empowers us to exhibit the political virtue of love.

I invite you now to pray the Cross Examen or the Cruciform Breath Prayer (explored in chapter 2), with special attention to how God's Spirit might be calling you and your faith community to embody the political virtue of love. In particular, ask the question: in what ways might God be calling you and your Christian community to "show up" or to "take a knee," to lose your old life and find abundant new life in, with, and for others, especially vulnerable others? Then, as in the Cross Examen or the Cruciform Breath Prayer, stay with this awareness throughout your activities this day, conscious of your deep interconnections with God, with everyone, and with everything, and compassionately and nonviolently resisting and transforming all that deforms human life and all creation.

5

Joy: The Second Political Virtue of the Spirit

I WAS SURPRISED WHEN I learned that Yale University had commenced a project to examine "joy." I don't know why I was surprised; people have been studying happiness for years, so why not joy? And according to the academic experts at Yale, joy is an emotion—not surprising, I think we knew that much. Joy also has an object, which makes sense because there must be an occasion or stimulus for it—a birth or a marriage, for instance. Moreover, joy has a moral dimension—that one gave me pause. Of course, morality can be corrupt, as when white supremacist David Duke said he was joyful when he heard a political candidate on a national stage espousing the same views that he had been promoting!

Yet joy can also be generous and attuned to suffering, emerging especially when suffering is relieved. Surprisingly, joy can be commanded. Finally, joy is a habit or virtue, which is to say that we can be formed to be joyful, which I found intriguing, especially in light of reflection on joy as a political virtue. In sum, as academics at Yale conduct consultations on joy, they are asking questions like these: Is joy naïve; i.e., is it too trusting, and do suspicions inhibit joy? Can joy be cultivated amid experiences of injustice?[1] Great questions! Theologian Willie Jennings, one of the consultants to the Yale study, defines joy as resistance to

1. "Theology of Joy." http://faith.yale.edu/joy/about.

despair.[2] I am intrigued by Jennings' comment because it brings us closer, I think, to Paul's notion of joy.

To get at Paul's understanding of joy, we need to review the theology and politics of Paul's letter to the Galatians and glance at other letters like 1 Thessalonians and Philippians, in which Paul speaks at length about joy. As we have seen, Paul's central theological and political claim in Galatians is that in the crucified and risen Christ alienating divisions and subordinations based in religion, gender, race, and class no longer pertain (Gal 3:28). When Paul insists, "I have been crucified with Christ; and it is no longer I who live, but Christ who lives in me" (Gal 2:19–20), he is asserting that the old self of alienating combative politics (which mimics the politics that crucified Jesus) is dissolved, dead, and washed away in baptism. As a result, there is, in Christ, what Brigitte Kahl refers to as a constant revolving and "revolutionary" movement from oneself to another.[3] This, in a nutshell, is what Paul is saying to the churches of Galatia.

Love, on this account, is cruciform—that is, cross-shaped, and defined in terms of dying and rising, or losing one's false self and retrieving a more authentic self in and with others. Joy is cruciform too, for it is linked to the retrieval of that fuller, more abundant self that is God's intention for us all. Thus Paul speaks of joy not as a transient emotion or "superficial cheerfulness," but as "a deep joy in what God has done in Christ and is continuing to do through the saints"—a joy that finds expression in sharing Christ's love and concern for others.[4] Indeed, joy is a shared reality, entailing mutuality: "One does not experience joy alone, but in the company of God's people."[5] Now think about that for a moment. What would you identify as moments that have been especially joyful for you? Most of us can name particular events that we remember as joyful (e.g., a birth or a marriage). But think also of those moments or encounters in which you found yourself caught up with others

2. "Theology of Joy." http://faith.yale.edu/joy/about.

3. Kahl, *Galatians Re-Imagined*, 269.

4. Hooker, "Philippians," 546.

5. Cousar, *Philippians and Philemon*, 85.

in a larger collective current or purpose that brought you in touch with something holy—something of the divine.

One such holy, joyful moment in my own life emerged during the Living Wage Campaign in Baltimore in 1992. It was an experience that I can only describe as cruciform joy, and one that will forever be imprinted on my memory and gives me goose bumps to this day. Member churches of the community organizing organization Baltimoreans United in Leadership Development (BUILD) had been working for over a year on the issue of low-income work in the city, and we were encountering stiff resistance from the mayor, the business community, and even some of our own church folk. But we pressed on because we saw people working for poverty-level wages. So one evening at a meeting attended by approximately 500 people (both low-wage workers and BUILD church members) we were strategizing about our next move. The workers shared that they had been threatened with job loss if they continued to work with BUILD on this campaign. The late Rev. Vernon Dobson, one of the founding members of BUILD, the longtime pastor of Union Baptist Church, and one of Baltimore's civil rights icons, encouraged the workers to stay the course. There seemed to be flames coming out of his fingers as he made a pledge to the workers: "If anyone threatens you again, all of the pastors in this room, all of the churches in BUILD represented here today, will stand with you—we will support you, so that they can't fire you, and we will make sure that they don't threaten you again. And we will do that because you are all children of God!"

As I listened, I knew that no matter what tensions we might be facing in the city or in our congregations over our advocacy for a living wage, there was a higher calling. It was, for me, a calling to stand with workers no matter what the cost, and to continue to work for the day when every one of God's children has a job that enables them to create and sustain a life. It was about as joyous a moment as I can remember in my life, in that it was a collective experience of joy that can only be described as cruciform, for it entailed losing an isolated, apathetic self and retrieving a much fuller self in, with, and for others. And our work eventually succeeded in creating the first living wage bill in the country! This experience helped me to realize that joy can be found in the face of resistance, even threatened persecution—as was the case when Paul spoke of joy in his first letter to the church at Thessalonica—a church well acquainted with the reality of joy in the face of persecution (1 Thess 1:6).

Moreover, the Apostle Paul speaks of joy as a mind-set, or what I would call a virtue, in Philippians 2. In what some have called Paul's "master story" of God and the world,[6] Paul tells the Philippian church:

> If then there is any encouragement in Christ, any conso-
> lation from love, any sharing in the Spirit, any compas-
> sion and sympathy, *make my joy complete: be of the same*
> *mind,* having the same love, being in full accord and of
> one mind. Do nothing from selfish ambition or conceit,
> but in humility regard others as better than yourselves.
> Let each of you look not to your own interests, but to
> the interests of others. Let the same mind be in you that
> was in Christ Jesus,
>
> who, though he was in the form of God,
> did not regard equality with God
> as something to be exploited,
> but emptied himself,
> taking the form of a slave,
> being born in human likeness.
> And being found in human form,
> he humbled himself
> and became obedient to the point of death—
> even death on a cross.
> Therefore God also highly exalted him
> and gave him the name
> that is above every name,
> so that at the name of Jesus
> every knee should bend,
> in heaven and on earth and under the earth,

6. Gorman, *Inhabiting,* 9–39.

and every tongue should confess
that Jesus Christ is Lord,
to the glory of God the Father.

In this significant passage, Paul is talking about the same cruciform joy of which he speaks in Galatians and Thessalonians, except here he speaks not only of our movement towards one another, but also of God's movement towards us—a movement of decidedly "downward mobility"[7] in which God's own self was emptied in order to transform, redeem, and liberate the world. This divine movement of love towards the world, in the world, with the world, and for the world is the very power of God. It is, for Paul, an occasion for the mind-set of joy. In fact, Paul speaks of joy more in Philippians than in any other letter, a letter penned, ironically, in a prison cell—underlining the fact that cruciform joy can emerge even in threatening circumstances. Indeed, joy (as it finds expression in Philippians) is "high paradoxical: it appears when it is least expected—in times of trial and struggle."[8] God's movement of decidedly downward mobility, in, with, and for the whole creation, seeks to break down the oppositional politics of the world.

We, too, are summoned to lives of downward mobility in Christ, in order to lose a false, abusive sense of ourselves and retrieve a more authentic sense of ourselves in, with, and for others—especially vulnerable others. And there may be no doubt that Paul perceived the Galatians as vulnerable. That is why he tells the Galatians churches to "bear one another's burdens, and in this way you will fulfill the law of Christ" (Gal 6:2). Brigitte Kahl claims that, for Paul, God's Spirit empowers "mindfulness in discerning, disobeying, and unfreezing" alienating, combative us-versus-them politics "that is set in stone and cast in iron everywhere; that imprisons and deforms every human being under the regimen."[9] Resistance to, and transformation of, all such politics is always an occasion for the mind-set and virtue of joy!

7. Gorman, *Inhabiting,* 9–39.
8. Cousar, *Philippians and Philemon,* 84.
9. Kahl, *Galatians Re-Imagined,* 269.

As I ponder the joy that emerges in the midst of resistance to, and transformation of, the realities of our lives that imprison and deform us, a remarkable person comes to mind, one I came to know in association with the homeless programs of the New York Avenue Presbyterian Church noted in the preceding chapter. His name is Charles, and I was introduced to him by Doug, a deacon who helps direct the congregation's ministries to the homeless. Some months before I personally met Charles, Doug had told me about an unusual person who was showing up on Sunday mornings for our breakfast program for the homeless. Charles, as Doug described him, was very quiet and non-assertive, standing by himself most of the time. Doug had to go out of his way to meet Charles, but when he did so, he was impressed, as was I. He was very articulate when asked a question, but seldom put himself forward.

When Charles eventually opened up, he told us that he had committed a crime in his late teens and had spent most of the last forty years of his life in prison. While incarcerated, he matured. He earned his high school equivalency degree and then went on to earn a college degree—he brought both of his diplomas to our Jobs Club meeting one day, and you could tell that he was proud of his achievements, as he should have been. He also started a chapter of the NAACP in his prison and served for many years as the chairperson of the organization. But when he was released from prison, life became very hard for Charles. On account of his disenfranchised status as a returning citizen, he found it nearly impossible to find a steady job, and thus spent most of his time on the streets of DC. With Doug's assistance, Charles finally secured a safe place to live, and our jobs program helped him start a lawn care and gardening business. One of our technology-savvy church members helped him develop a website to attract and secure clients. Doug then facilitated the process of buying a car so that Charles could transport himself and his equipment to work sites. To be sure, life was still very hard for Charles, but you could also tell that he had a new sense of purpose and hope. Using Brigitte Kahl's terminology, Charles was "unfreezing" the combative world that continued to seek to imprison him in his past. All of us who have had the privilege of knowing and working with Charles have shared in that joy—a collective experience of cruciform, or life-out-of-death, joy! Joy is indeed a mutual reality, shared in the company of God's people as they participate in God's resurrecting work in the world.

I invite you again to pray the Cross Examen or the Cruciform Breath Prayer with special attention to how God's Spirit might be calling you and your faith community to embody the political virtue of joy. As you pray, recall especially those moments in which you have sensed that you were being caught up in something larger than yourself—holy experiences of standing with the vulnerable, the oppressed, or for a just cause that was an occasion for what could be called cruciform joy. Then, as in the Cross Examen or the Cruciform Breath Prayer, stay with this awareness throughout your activities this day, conscious of your interconnections with God, with everyone, and with everything, compassionately and nonviolently resisting and transforming all that deforms human life and all creation.

6

Peace: The Third Political Fruit of the Spirit

IN PAUL'S LETTERS, THE word *peace* invariably appears in his introductory greetings to recipients. Thus in Galatians, these are among the opening words: "Grace to you and *peace* from God our Father and the Lord Jesus Christ, who gave himself for our sins and delivered us from the present evil age" (Gal 1:3). This verse captures, in a nutshell, a summary of the letter and in many respects Paul's entire theology: peace is a gift we receive *not* from Caesar, but from God, who in Jesus Christ has liberated us from the present evil age in which Caesar reigns through a "law and order" campaign. Modern politicos were not the first to coin "law and order" rhetoric; Caesar ruled on its foundation, and Pharaoh before him, long before politicians in our own time and place took up this banner. Indeed, Caesar imposed it and literally crucified everyone that got in the way. This was the means through which Caesar sustained the much vaunted "Pax Romana"—which to Paul's way of thinking was no peace at all.

Though times have changed, crosses still litter the landscape of our world. Consider one all too egregious example: the mass incarceration of black men in American society—what Michelle Alexander has aptly dubbed "the new Jim Crow."[1] This is but one illustration of what "peace" purports to look like when Caesar's "law and order" campaign reigns. Paul has an alternative vision. Peace, for Paul, is cruciform, which is to say that it is grounded in

1. Alexander, *The New Jim Crow*.

the cross of Jesus by which he, and we, have been crucified by, and to, Caesar's world and Caesar's ways, in order that we might live by the power of resurrection as a beachhead of a new creation. As Paul insists in Galatians, "May I never boast of anything except *the cross of our Lord Jesus Christ, by which the world has been crucified to me,* and I to the world. For neither circumcision nor uncircumcision is anything; but *a new creation is everything!* As for those who will follow this rule—*peace* be upon them, and mercy" (Gal 6:14–16). As we are baptized into Christ's death, the grip and inscriptions upon us of Caesar's world and Caesar's ways have been washed away in the waters of baptism.

In short, Paul perceived the cross of Jesus Christ as the true source of peace. As New Testament scholar Robert Jewett points out, the argument for Paul boiled down to a choice between Christ or Caesar—to discern "which gospel has the power to make the world truly peaceful."[2] The cross—though intended by the Romans to impose law and order and to keep all the hierarchies of wealth, religion, and gender in place—is for Paul a revolutionary birth canal for the new creation. As we are baptized into Christ's death, washed in baptismal waters, we are crucified to all that deforms and defaces our lives, and freed to find more abundant selves in, with, and for others—especially vulnerable others.

Peace thus entails "reconciliation" with others with whom we are at enmity; so to get at Paul's understanding of peace as a fruit of the Spirit one has to consider also his understanding of "reconciliation"—which many would argue is the metaphor at the center of Paul's theology. Reconciliation language appears primarily in Paul's letters in the New Testament (see especially Rom 5:9–10 and 2 Cor 5:14–21), and the basic meaning of the word group is this: "changing an enemy into a friend."[3] It conveys a change in social relationship in which two parties previously at enmity with each other exchange friendship and peace. It also bears the sense of exchanging places with the other—of being in solidarity with the other rather than against the other—of being

2. Quoted in Elliott, *The Arrogance*, 73.
3. Countryman, "Reconcile, Reconciliation," 410.

able to stand in someone else's shoes. It is important to note that in Paul's view, God, through the crucified and risen Christ, takes all of the initiative in removing hostility and in making those who were enemies into friends—in reconciling us with ourselves, with others, with the earth itself, and with God's own self! As Paul affirms in 2 Corinthians 5:17-18, "So if anyone is in Christ, there is a new creation: everything old has passed away; see, everything has become new! All this is from God, who reconciled us to himself through Christ, and has given us the ministry of reconciliation." It is also important to note that God is always the subject, rather than the object, of reconciliation language, for "it is not God who needs to be reconciled to humans, but humans who need reconciliation with God."[4] And once reconciled with God, we are entrusted with the "ministry of reconciliation," with partnership in God's own reconciling, peacemaking work in the human community and all of creation.

The Spirit's fruit of peace is also closely connected to what Israel's prophets spoke of, in Hebrew, as *shalom*—a vision of wholeness and human flourishing that entailed justice as well as peace. So as we reflect on reconciliation and the peace it establishes, it also needs to be said that talk about peace as reconciliation can ring hollow, especially if it does not have a justice-seeking and justice-creating core. Peace, in other words, is not cruciform peace unless it confronts and seeks transformation of the deformations of our world. Peace that is not mediated through justice is deceitful. As an example, Allan Boesak tells of his encounter with five young black South Africans disillusioned by glib talk of reconciliation, when he arrived for a meeting at the Apartheid Museum in Johannesburg in late 2001:

> They knew I was coming, and they must have been waiting for me. . . . It turned out to be a discussion about reconciliation that, the young people felt, "was not working." They explained that what might be a good thing for white people was not such a good thing for blacks after all. "In the townships where we live," they explained,

4. Cousar, *The Letters of Paul*, 126.

"nothing had come of it, and nothing was seen of it."
They felt that white people "just did not care" and had
not shown they understood what black people had suffered under apartheid, what it cost to offer the hand of
friendship and forgiveness that was now being "slapped
away." "We are being wasted," they said, meaning "we,
as persons," their past, their struggle, their feelings, their
willingness to make it work, their faith that it must work.[5]

Boesak's story prompts us to reflect on pursuits in our own country and communities—many of which have no doubt failed to
bear fruit because they were empty gestures of peace; confessions
and declarations of forgiveness that did not lead to real healing,
restoration, and reparations. Indeed, civil rights icon Ruby Sales
says something that I, as a white person, need to hear—that perhaps we all need to hear:

[T]here's a spiritual crisis in white America. It's a crisis
of meaning. . . . [W]e talk a lot about black theologies,
but I want a liberating white theology. I want a theology
that speaks to Appalachia. I want a theology that begins
to deepen people's understanding about their capacity to
live fully human lives and to touch the goodness inside of
them rather than call upon the part of themselves that's
not relational. Because there's nothing wrong with being
European American. That's not the problem. It's how you
actualize that history and how you actualize that reality.
It's almost like white people don't believe that other white
people are worthy of being redeemed. And I don't quite
understand that. It must be more sexy to deal with black
folk than it is to deal with white folk if you're a white
person. So as a black person, I want a theology that gives
hope and meaning to people who are struggling to have
meaning in a world where they no longer are as essential
to whiteness as they once were.[6]

A liberating white theology—white folk are surely in need
of it. And what might that mean? As I sought an answer to that

5. Boesak and DeYoung, *Radical Reconciliation*, 151.
6. Tippett and Sales, "Where Does It Hurt?"

question, I found myself returning again and again to a haunting quote from James Cone at the end of his extraordinary book, *The Cross and the Lynching Tree*. Cone claims that "[w]hen whites lynched blacks, they were literally lynching themselves—their sons, daughters, cousins."[7] Initially I was flummoxed by this statement. I had to think long and hard about it—and I'm still trying to fully wrap my head around it. My tentative understanding is that James Cone, like Paul, is contending that ideologies of supremacy deform *all* of us—both the crucifiers and the crucified. Both crucifiers and the crucified are disfigured by enmity. Both crucifiers and the crucified bear wounds. The wounds of the oppressed and of their privileged oppressors are, to be sure, different in degree and kind, but they are nonetheless wounds that must be acknowledged and named in order to be healed.

In fact, Luke Bretherton poignantly contends that pondering the wounds of the crucified Christ can be the critical opening that enables the privileged to grasp their solidarity with the oppressed. Contemplating Christ, he says, can lead to repentance, reparation, and a disruption of what one sees. It is "proximity to Christ on the cross that determines who and what we should see. Uncoupled from the contemplation of Christ crucified, the privileged will miscategorize what suffering looks like and who is the stranger to be welcomed."[8] But when the privileged contemplate the wounded Christ "so that they might be provoked to repent and to understand both their own 'poverty'/sinfulness and their need for a meaningful relationship with the destitute, afflicted, and powerless . . . [they] become open to the realization that they have a common life, in and through Christ, with the poor. 'We' cannot be healed without 'them,' nor they without us."[9] In other words, examining our collective brokenness in Christ can lead to life together as "wounded healers."[10]

---

7. Cone, *The Cross*, 165.

8. Bretherton, *Christ and the Common Life*, 69

9. Bretherton, *Christ and the Common Life*, 68

10. This phrase is borrowed from Nouwen, *The Wounded Healer*.

In his concluding remarks to the churches of Galatia, Paul declares "I carry the marks of Jesus branded on my body" (Gal 6:17), which is, I think, a way of saying that we are all crucified, but that God in Christ has confronted, liberated, redeemed, and healed us, though we still bear the marks of the nails. Caesar's world and Caesar's ways have left scars upon us all; still, "if anyone is in Christ, there is a new creation: everything old has passed away; see, everything has become new!" (2 Cor 5:17). So the question before us, then, as Ruby Sales puts it, is "how you actualize that reality." What are we going to act on?

In good Pauline fashion, Bob Dylan states the choice before us succinctly in a classic song: "you're gonna have to serve somebody . . . it may be the devil, or it may be the Lord, but you're gonna have to serve somebody." So which will it be? The stigmata of Caesar are on us and in us, and we can act on them; or, by the power of the Spirit of the crucified and risen Christ in whom we have been baptized, we can be washed clean, liberated, and freed from the chains of enslavement to violence and enmity in order to live out of the image of God in us by being with, in, and for one another in love. As theologian Brian Bantum astutely observes: "Race is the lie that I can be who I am, without you. Race is a system that makes some people's thriving contingent on other people's dehumanization. Christian discipleship is the confession that I am not me without you, and that our community is not whole while some are perpetually diminished."[11]

It is important to note that the new community of disciples birthed by the cross and resurrection is washed clean of enslavement to violence and enmity, but it is *not* washed clean of difference. To return to Paul's baptismal affirmation in Galatians 3:28: when he affirms that "there is neither Jew nor Gentile, neither slave nor free, nor is there male and female, for you are all one in Christ Jesus," he does not envision erasure of difference, because difference is an essential part of God's good creation. Rather, Paul wants Jews as Jews standing in mutuality with Gentiles as Gentiles—with no enmity between them, repairing the harm created by enmity.

11. Bantum, *The Death of Race*, 103.

Indeed, this is the sign of new creation that the church embodies in the world and that is essential to its public witness.

A covenant community in which difference is not erased: this is what the fruit of peace, embodied, looks like—a peace "surpassing all understanding" (Phil 4:7) because it is not like any peace that the world gives. It is a peace that faces directly into Caesar's reign in order to overcome, redeem, liberate, wash it clean of violence and repair the harm. It is peace grounded in reconciliation with the cruciform God of love who frees us to live fully with, in, and for others and ourselves. It is a peace that liberates us from all ideologies of supremacy (including whiteness) that deform and deface us all. In sum, the peace that signals new creation—the *shalom* or wholeness that God intends for all—entails choosing and celebrating difference. Brian Bantum articulates this eloquently:

> When God created us, God created us to be like God. God wanted us to love and to be loved. But when you love someone you have to choose them. You have to choose them in the big things and in the small things. To love someone you have to see how they are like you and how they are not like you, and you have to see how their differences are gifts, ways of helping you to see yourself and God and the world in new ways. We were made like fountains that are always being filled by a stream of living water and pouring out into the other fountains around us. We are always being filled and we are always pouring out. That's what it means to be made in God's image. . . . Our lives are made whole in these differences. Difference is the opportunity to choose one another and to choose God.[12]

It bears repeating: the peace that breaks down hierarchies of privilege in order to reconcile difference can never be truly cruciform peace unless it also entails reparation for harm that has been inflicted. Indeed, ethicist Jennifer Harvey contends that the only way Americans will ever live into racial reconciliation will be to abandon the reconciliation paradigm itself in order to fully

12. Bantum, *The Death of Race*, 50–51.

embrace reparations for harm caused by histories of racism in this country.[13] As much as I appreciate Harvey's observation, I am not ready to abandon "reconciliation" as a worthy goal because I believe it is grounded in cruciform peace that demands accountability for harm and participation in restorative justice. In other words, reparation for harm goes hand in hand with the embrace and celebration of difference—else it is no peace at all.

One of my favorite celebrations during the Christian year has always been World Communion Sunday—a liturgical occasion on which peace, a distinctive fruit of the Spirit, and celebration of the rich diversity that is God's gift to us, find unique expression. In all the congregations I have served, we have placed different kinds of bread from around the world on the communion table on this Sunday to represent the diversity that is clearly God's intent for our lives. This celebration reminds us that whenever we make difference an occasion for enmity and strife or for hierarchies of privilege—when we make difference an occasion to rank and order God's goodness—we deface what God intends for us and fail to embody the divine gift of peace. On World Communion Sunday, when we come to the table as one with Christians from around the world, we live ever more fully into new creation. As we come together at the table with all our differences, the Spirit of the crucified and risen Christ is at work in us, teaching us how to embody the fruit of the Spirit that is peace.

I invite you to pray the Cross Examen or the Cruciform Breath Prayer with special attention to how God's Spirit might be calling you and your faith community to embody peace, a fruit of the Spirit that is a public, political virtue. As you pray, ponder deeply the enmities that find expression in your life and your community, whatever their source. What differences are at the heart of the enmities you discern. Reflect on and name the crucifying effects of these differences and the marks they have left on you and others. Reflect also on how God might be at work in you, nudging friendship, peace, and justice-seeking restoration and reparation amid these divisions. Then, as in the Cross Examen or

13. Harvey, *Dear White Christians*, 253.

the Cruciform Breath Prayer, stay with this awareness throughout your activities this day, conscious of your interconnections with God, with everyone, and with everything, compassionately and nonviolently resisting and transforming realities that deform human life and all creation.

7

Patience: The Fourth Political Fruit of the Spirit

MUCH OF WHAT I have learned about the political fruit of patience emerged from my engagement in Baltimore's Living Wage Campaign. As I've noted before, in the fall of 1992 the churches of BUILD (Baltimoreans United In Leadership Development) embarked on this campaign to address the issue of low-income work in Baltimore. My introduction to the issue began in predawn hours, standing outside of a fast food joint called "Mr. J's," where underemployed folk hung out to eat breakfast and fill out applications for work at TOPS (Temporary Overload Placement Systems), a temporary work organization in Baltimore. Jonathan Lange, one of the BUILD organizers, prepared us for the morning's event. We learned that TOPS is an organization that contracts with Baltimore construction companies, housing complexes, plants of all kinds, and even the state of Maryland. Yet whatever the location, the work is the same—it is work that no one else will do: cleaning up, clearing trash, heavy lifting, and digging ditches. It is the kind of burdensome work that contractors will not subject their full-time employees to, so they contract with TOPS.

The way it works is this: a contractor will pay TOPS between $10 to $14 an hour for each worker. This is, of course, an advantage for the contractor, because they do not have to pay benefits and they do not have to fool with part-time employees. TOPS then turns around and pays their workers $4.25 an hour (the minimum wage in 1992). So somebody is making a profit off this deal, but it does not flow to the workers. Jonathan then explained that we were going into Mr. J's to talk with folk and find out what it is like working with TOPS. With these instructions, we made our way through the crowd at Mr. J's.

I bought a cup of coffee and caught the eye an older gentleman sitting close to where I was standing. He had a smile on his face, so I sat down and introduced myself. His name was Ripley— or Rip as he liked to be called. Rip was a friendly man with kind eyes, in his late fifties or early sixties—not old enough for a social security check, but too old for the heavy kind of work he was doing. He was very open with me, and his story shook me to the core. He had worked multiple jobs in a variety of settings—as a waiter at a country club and in the laundry service of the Embassy Hotel in Hunt Valley (an exclusive part of Baltimore County). Yet the most he ever earned in his life was $6 an hour; and every time he had made enough money to live on, he got laid off. But he had never been on public assistance; he had always worked, and he wanted to work! And I couldn't help but think to myself, here is someone who is working for his poverty—he can barely pay the rent. At TOPS, Rip makes $138 a week, hardly enough to keep him housed and put a little food on the table. He often goes to local soup kitchens and food pantries because it saves on the food bill. Finally, I asked him the question that tugged at my heart: "How do you keep going?" Rip smiled, looked skywards, and said, "God helps me, God helps me!"

As Rip spoke, words of Jesus came to mind: "Come, you that are blessed by my Father, inherit the kingdom prepared for you from the foundation of the world; for I was hungry and you gave me food, I was thirsty and you gave me something to drink, I was a stranger and you welcomed me" (Matt 25:35–36). Rip is a man who finds welcome in our soup kitchens, but he has not been fully welcomed in our society. And it is noteworthy that these words of Jesus, from his most evocative judgment scene, are addressed not to individuals, but to "the nations" who will be gathered before the throne and separated, "as a shepherd separates the sheep from the goats." It is the nations who will be judged on the basis of whether or not they have welcomed people like Rip, for Jesus also said,

"Truly I tell you, just as you did it to one of the least of these who are members of my family, you did it to me" (Matt 25:40). How can we as a people fail to see that Christ is truly present in the predawn hours of a Baltimore morning? Christ comes to us in every human being who crosses our paths, who torments our conscience or demands our attention. Christ is sleeping over heating grates on cold winter mornings. He returns at the end of a workday to a solitary room, or maybe he has no room at all and grows old and lonely, unwanted and unkempt. Christ squats alone and afraid on every corner of our world. We try not to look for fear that something will be asked of us, but Christ is there. Without a doubt, I encountered Christ in Rip in the predawn hours in 1992, as he filled out his application for yet another day's work.

To put it bluntly, meeting Rip and learning about his work history and employment situation with a contemptible organization like TOPS—challenges shared by countless others in our country's low-income work force—made me angry. But one thing that I have learned about anger through community organizing is this: there is bad anger and there is good anger. Bad anger can destroy or warp our perceptions of others, our circumstances, and ourselves; but good anger can motivate us to do something constructive and creative about injustice, oppression, and violence. Good anger is what community organizers call "cold anger." Mary Beth Rogers defines cold anger as direct experience of dehumanizing injustice that "transforms itself into compassion for those hurt. . . . It is the kind of anger that can energize democracy—because it can lead to the first step in changing politics."[1]

Cold anger, I contend, has a symbiotic relationship to the political virtue of patience—the fourth fruit of the Spirit of which Paul speaks in Gal 5:22. Interestingly, the Greek word for "patience" that Paul uses is *makrothymia*, a word that is comprised of two component parts: *makro*, which means "long or extended" and *thymia*, which means to "temper"—which suggests that the word can mean "long tempered" or "forbearing." Paul uses this same word in Romans 9:22–24 to describe how God's justified anger at Israel

---

1. Rogers, *Cold Anger,* 9–10.

is tempered ("endured with much patience") in order to offer the opportunity for change or transformation. This description of the relation between anger and patience is very close to the definition of cold anger cited above; i.e., hot anger tempered or transformed into compassion and directed toward change. Consider also how Paul, in contrasting "works of the flesh" with "fruit of the Spirit," juxtaposes death-tending, crucifying anger (a work of the flesh, Gal 5:19) with patience (a Spirit-empowered fruit or virtue, Gal 5:22)—which further suggests that anger can be tempered for the purpose of change and transformation. Indeed, I would contend that patience is by no means a passive virtue as often supposed, but rather an active, passionate virtue that reshapes emotions like anger for positive change. Patience thus can mean "learning how to turn . . . hot burning anger down a notch or two and make it cold, controlled, and careful, guiding it like some swift, sure missile homing [in] on its target."[2]

In the context of Galatians and Paul's theology of the cross, patience (like the virtues that precede and follow it in Paul's catalogue of fruit of the Spirit) is a cruciform virtue. After listing the fruit of the Spirit, Paul declares that "those who belong to Christ Jesus have crucified the flesh with its passions and desires" (Gal 5:24)—and it is critical to understand what Paul's notion of the "flesh" that is crucified does—and does not—mean. As Ched Myers and Elaine Enns explain, "flesh" is not a reference to sexual passion (as commonly misunderstood). It conveys rather a "deeply rooted, socially conditioned worldview"—like a prejudice that one inherits.[3] The "flesh," in other words, is a socially deforming worldview that is imbibed from the dominant culture. This interpretation helps make sense of one of Paul's identified works of the flesh: idolatry (Gal 5:20). The idolatry of which he speaks surely includes ethnocentricism, that is, the privileging (divinizing) of one ethnic group over against another—privileging that Paul, in his letter to the Galatians, fiercely rejects. One does not have to look far for expressions of ethnocentrism in our own time and place,

2. Rogers, *Cold Anger*, 39.

3. Myers and Enns, *Ambassadors of Reconciliation*, 10.

as they are sadly pervasive; but a particularly notable example was provided by President Donald J. Trump's outrageously racist declaration (on July 13, 2019) that four minority US congresswomen should "go back and help fix the broken and crime infested places from which they came." This comment received widespread attention, for only one of the four congresswomen was born in a foreign country—and all are US citizens, duly elected to Congress! Sadly, Trump's words reflect a long-standing assumption shared by a number of Americans: that the United States is destined by God to be a racially pure (i.e., white, European American) nation.[4] Paul would have been aghast at such an assumption, for its ethnocentrism bears similarities to the false gospel he decried in his letter to the Galatian churches.

The good news Paul proclaims is that "those who belong to Christ have crucified the flesh," which entails any and all such deceptions. The good news is also that by the powerful Spirit of the crucified and risen Christ at work within us, they can be transformed into fruit that facilitates positive engagement with the world around us. Hot, destructive anger can be transformed into cold, targeted anger that engenders change. Indeed, Paul's own hot anger and violence against the early followers of Jesus was crucified and transformed into a passionate mission to the crucified. Cold anger (via cruciform patience) can be described as the power to stand with, in, and for the crucified with confidence in God's resurrecting power, without acquiescing to the violent idolatrous powers that deform and deface us all. Cruciform patience resists and seeks the transformation of idolatrous deceptions, creating the space for change. Theologian James Cone describes the black religious experience in America in a way that captures the concept of cruciform patience:

> The real scandal of the gospel is this: humanity's salvation is revealed in the cross of the condemned criminal Jesus, and humanity's salvation is available only through our solidarity with the crucified people in our midst. Faith that emerged out of the scandal of the cross is not

4. See Douglas, *Stand Your Ground,* chapter 3.

a faith of intellectuals or elites of any sort. This is the faith of abused and scandalized people—the losers and the down and out. It was this faith that gave blacks the strength and courage to hope, "to keep on keeping on," struggling against the odds, with what Paul Tillich called "the courage to be."[5]

Cone's conception of "salvation" as solidarity with crucified people and of "faith" as the strength to stay in the struggle requires the patience of which Paul speaks in Galatians as a distinctive fruit of the Spirit—anticipatory patience that awaits the transformation of works of the flesh like "anger" into the courage and energy to incite change. Indeed, the noted community organizer Ernesto Cortez searches for people who are angry, because he knows that anger can stir up compassion for others that can be transformed into political action. Anger, after all, is energy, and energy is needed for change to occur. "Anger," he says, "is something very deep and it is rooted in memory. . . . It's not just a spur-of-the-moment kind of thing. It is tied to loss, grief, and it is rooted in relationship and concerns with other people."[6] Clearly implied in Cortez's comments about anger, and its transformation into compassionate relation with others, is the power of love. Indeed, cruciform patience is grounded in love, the foundational fruit of the Spirit. Love, as we have noted, entails the virtue of "showing up" in solidarity with others, which plays an essential role in transforming anger into constructive, collective energy for the common good.

I recently encountered the embodiment of cruciform patience and love in a Christian community in Ghana that I will never forget. I was co-leading a bi-annual travel seminar from Union Presbyterian Seminary, which immersed us in a rich learning experience about the religion, culture, and history of that West African country. The congregation we visited on one of our final days in Ghana was situated in Agbogbloshie, a slum in the heart of Accra on the banks of the Korle Lagoon—a slum that has achieved notoriety as one of the most polluted in the world,

5. Cone, *The Cross*, 160.
6. Rogers, *Cold Anger*, 189–90.

hosting one of its largest electronics waste dumps. Agbogbloshie is populated by roughly 40,000 migrants from the Sub-Saharan north and rural areas who have journeyed south to Accra, fleeing tribal conflict in northern Ghana with the hope of finding safety, food, jobs, resources. But hopes have largely been dashed, for the only place they have found to live is amidst the harsh living conditions and rampant crime of one of Accra's largest slums and its hot, crowded market for the selling of yams imported from northern Ghana and onions from Nigeria.

The church we visited in Agbogbloshie was the Konkomba Market Congregation of the Evangelical Presbyterian Church of Ghana. It was planted to nourish life and community in an otherwise bleak world and it was clear that their mission was being accomplished. About twenty members of the church came to our late morning gathering for conversation with us. They extended extraordinary hospitality, even a meal of northern yams that we shared on their communion table. They also sang and danced for us, providing an opportunity for us to experience tribal dances from the north that we had not seen during our time in Ghana.

During a question and answer period, one member of our group asked about the core message of the church and, without hesitation, Presbyter Solomon responded: "to love God and neighbor as yourself." I wondered if loving God and neighbor entailed a political edge, so I asked if the city officials of Accra ever addressed the needs of their community. The answer was yes—politicians promise aid and infrastructure, but those promises are never acted on. So I asked a follow-up question: "Does that make you angry?" The answer was immediate: "Yes, lots of us are angry!"

I found both of these answers heartening—for love and anger, as we have seen, are the key ingredients for engendering transformation. If the political virtue of love calls us "to show up," to lose our old life and find it more abundantly in, with, and for others, especially vulnerable others, then anger, channeled by cruciform patience, can energize democracy—it can animate the staying power that enables change. Anger and love are the key ingredients for change. Love of God and neighbor along with targeted anger reflect the collective desire to fight adversity, engendering hope for a better life. Both were on full display that day in Agbogbloshie, for the Konkomba Market Congregation is vitally engaged in mission; indeed, they shared ambitious plans to add a second story to their one-story building in order to house a medical clinic for their neighborhood. The congregation, in other words, is an embodiment of love and anger in action!

As you have no doubt gathered from previous chapters, one of my proudest memories will always be my participation, and that of my congregation, with BUILD in the Living Wage Campaign in Baltimore where, in the mid-1990s, we fought for, and helped to pass, the first living wage bill for city service workers in the country. The bill elevated city service contracts from minimum wage to $9 an hour including benefits—a significant achievement in the mid-1990s. This bill has since been replicated in over thirty cities around the country, including New York. It did not happen overnight. Nor will change happen overnight for the Konkomba Market Congregation of Ghana. But in this we can trust: in places of crucifixion God's resurrecting power is already at work, bringing life out of death. The transformative power of the Spirit of the crucified and risen Christ is turning hot anger, via cruciform patience, into energy to show up and to stand with, in, and for the crucified, resisting the crucifixions of our neighborhoods and world. For me as a Christian, this work demands a patience born of the Spirit of Christ who continues to empower us to embody God's new creation.

I invite you now to pray the Cross Examen or the Cruciform Breath Prayer (explored in chapter 3) with special attention to how God's Spirit might be calling you and your faith community to embody the political virtue of patience. As you pray, ponder deeply and name the hot anger in your life that can be channeled into cold, patient anger—the kind of anger that shows up, stands with the oppressed, and resists the crucifixions of the world. Then, as in the Cross Examen or the Cruciform Breath Prayer, stay with this awareness throughout your activities this day, conscious of your interconnections with God, with everyone, and with everything, compassionately and nonviolently resisting and transforming all that deforms human life and all creation.

8

Kindness: The Fifth Political Fruit of the Spirit

ALICE ROSE TEWELL, MY former colleague in ministry, once asked me to recommend a spiritual practice that the children and youth in our congregation could engage during Sunday School and in their daily lives, and I immediately thought of the breath prayer described in chapter 2. It is the simplest and most profound prayer I know, and I have used a simplified version of this prayer with children many times. The breath prayer has been part of my spiritual practice for years. I learned it from Zen Buddhist monk Thich Nhat Hanh as a form of mindfulness attuned to our most basic interconnectedness with all that is.[1] In his fine book *Fruit of the Spirit*, Franciscan monk Michael Crosby references Nhat Hanh, recommending the breath prayer as a practice that cultivates the mystical foundation needed for nurturing the varied fruit of the Spirit:

> I am convinced that the discipline of developing a mystical stance begins with becoming conscious or mindful or aware of one's breathing. This is not only good for daily living but is a basic discipline for cultivating a more mystical consciousness. And well it should be, for the Spirit of God . . . is the "breath of God." When we practice deep breathing, we discipline ourselves to become conscious of our connectedness "in Christ," which links us to everyone and everything in the cosmos. In this way we are aware of a new creation that is evolving into ever-greater forms of communion and love.

1. See, for example, Hanh, *Breathe.*

Here there is no more separation, only connectedness. In breathing in, I breathe in everyone and everything in a way that should make me an embodiment of the new creation. In breathing out, I release from myself and my control anything that may be an obstacle to the grace of the Spirit breathing in me. The practice of such breathing helps move one into a deeper consciousness of the Holy Spirit as the source of what N. T. Wright calls our "incorporation" and "participation" in the body of Christ. While this consciousness or "mindfulness," a Buddhist like Thich Nhat Hanh can declare, "is very much like the Holy Spirit"; it is much more if it is nurtured by actually growing in mystical prayer itself.[2]

It seems to me that the breath prayer has special relevance for reflection on the Spirit's fruit of kindness, for the breath prayer, like kindness, creates the space for deep, compassionate pondering of our interrelationship with everyone and all creation. In Hebrew, the word for kindness is *hesed*; in Greek it is *chrēstotēs*. The sense in which Paul uses *chrēstotēs* is apparent in Romans 2:4 when he asks: "Or do you despise the riches of God's kindness and forbearance and patience? Do you not realize that God's kindness is meant to lead you to repentance?" Interestingly, in 1 Corinthians 13, he again connects *chrēstotēs* (or kindness) to patience when he notes that "Love is patient; love is kind" (1 Cor 13:4).

This connection between kindness and patience reflects its Hebrew origin in *hesed*, a term especially descriptive of God's covenant with Israel. God's *hesed* or loving kindness is on full display in the classic story of the golden calf in the book of Exodus. Even in the wake of Israel's betrayal, God is "merciful and gracious, slow to anger, and abounding in steadfast love (*hesed*) and faithfulness, keeping steadfast love (*hesed*) for the thousandth generation" (Exod 34:6-7). Kindness (whether *chrēstotēs* in Greek or *hesed* in Hebrew) is thus an expansive concept that embraces love, mercy, patience, and the withholding of anger—all in one word. It is perhaps the most uncommon of virtues in a deeply polarized world such as ours where tit for tat violence reigns and combative,

2. Crosby, *Fruit*, 106.

divisive rhetoric dominates the airwaves. How are we to live into this virtue in our time and place?

A starting point for reflection may be provided by the very etymology of the word, for as British theologian Janet Martin Soskice notes in her book on *The Kindness of God*, "In Middle English the words 'kind' and 'kin' were the same—to say that Christ is 'our kinde Lord' is not to say that Christ is tender and gentle, although that may be implied, but to say that he is kin—our kind."[3] But the connection between kindness and kin raises immediate questions. We usually assume that we should be kind to our kin, that is, to our immediate and extended family, but who, in fact, are our kin? Is the circle of kin restricted to our family, our ethnicity, our national compatriots, or our racialized identity? The same interpretive question is raised by the great commandment to love God and neighbor: who exactly is my neighbor? (A question we will explore in the next chapter.) But it is worth noting that in verses that immediately precede Paul's discussion of the fruit of the Spirit, he affirms that the whole law of God is summed up in "loving neighbor as oneself" and "bearing one another's burdens" (Gal 5:14; 6:2).

Moreover, given the severity of the ecological crisis that we now face, should not the earth, too, be embraced as neighbor, indeed kin, deserving of our kindness? In a compelling essay, Ellen Davis highlights the fact that in biblical and agrarian perspective people and land are in fact related, as Genesis 2:7 affirms: "And the Lord God formed the human being [*adam*], dust from the fertile-soil [*adamah*]." As Davis notes, "We are 'descended,' so to speak, as *adam* from *adamah*. This is a rare instance where a Hebrew pun works: we are human from humus. People and land are kin."[4]

All these considerations surely point us toward the mystery of incarnation—the Christian notion that God became our "kind." As John's prologue affirms, "the Word became flesh and lived among us" (John 1:14). Interestingly, John does not say that "the Word became *human*," but rather that the "Word became *flesh*," which is a broader category, for humans are but one living

3. Quoted in Crosby, *Fruit*, 198.
4. Davis, "Land as Kin," 5.

species. The Word became an earth creature, dependent on a dense web of biodiversity: "God's incarnation became a deep incarnation into the fleshly biological life of the earth."[5] Thus the divine incarnation means that we are deeply interconnected with God, with one another, and with God's whole creation. As Ian McFarland observes, "[I]ncarnation creates a situation in which the whole material realm" is "pressed into the service of imaging God."[6] Yet if the whole material realm bears the image of God and thus kinship to us, the reality of climate change speaks of a great derangement of this relation.

Theologian Norman Wirzba references an alarming prediction by climate change experts, noting that by the end of the twenty-first century, Miami and other sea-level cities and nations around the world will have disappeared and tens of millions in the world will become climate refugees because of the rising of ocean levels. They also predict that climate change will result in massive starvation, drought, disease, and perpetual war for precious resources. What Wirzba notes is that we are now living in a new era described as the age of the Anthropocene—that is, a moment in history in which humans, rather than natural forces, have become the dominant force in our planet's history, changing land, ocean, and atmosphere. We are no longer at the mercy of nature, but rather have become the great predators of nature. We are, in other words, crucifiers of nature. What can be done? How can we uncrucify nature?

Wirzba contends that it is essential to see that "God's trajectory throughout Scripture has always been *toward* Earth rather than *away* from it. Christians need to reject all privatizing, escapist models of salvation and learn to participate in God's restoring and redeeming ways with the whole world."[7] This entails rediscovering our kinship with the earth and all who dwell in it, kindly and compassionately attending to creation's pain and sufferings.

5. Shore-Goss, "An Ecological Reading," 283.

6. McFarland, *The Divine Image*, 33.

7. Wirzba, "Waking Up to the Anthropocene," 22–27.

There is a further implication to consider: our enemies are included among those to whom the incarnate Christ, our "kin and kind," reconnects us. This is why Paul, in Romans, enjoins believers not to return evil for evil, but to overcome evil with good (Rom 12:14–21)—an admonition that resonates with that of the Matthean Jesus, who commands us to love our enemies (Matt 5:43–48). In fact, theologian Miroslav Volf claims that the notion of loving our enemies goes to the heart of the Christian faith:

> From the very start, at the center of Christian faith was some version of the claim that God loved the sinful world and . . . that Christ's followers must love their enemies no less than they love themselves. Love doesn't mean agreement and approval; it means benevolence and beneficence, possible disagreement and disapproval notwithstanding. A combination of moral clarity that does not shy away from calling evil by its proper name and of deep compassion toward evildoers that is willing to sacrifice one's own life on their behalf was one of the extraordinary features of early Christianity. It should also be the central characteristic of contemporary Christianity.[8]

Luke Bretherton, however, wisely cautions against any naiveté about enemy love, for it can easily lapse into romantic notions that too readily dissolve differences or fail to acknowledge how power differentials abuse and oppress the most vulnerable. As he notes, the "powerful mostly refuse to recognize they are enemies to the oppressed and claim they are friends with everyone." Moreover, the temptation of the powerful is to "fix the system so that they lose nothing and others always lose."[9] Thus loving one's enemies may require confrontation with them, in order to conscientize them to their abuse of power. In fact, in commmunity organizing, we follow the adage that in public relations there are "no permanent enemies and no permanent friends" because the tension between conflict and mediation—enemy and friend—is always dynamic and never fully resolved.

8. Volf, *A Public Faith*, 132.

9. Bretherton, *Christ and the Common Life*, 42–43.

Luke's story of Zacchaeus provides a paradigmatic account of enemy/friend dynamics. Zacchaeus was a rich, chief tax collector and all-around stooge for the Romans, and as such, he was hated by his own people—ostracized as a traitor. Community organizers conduct power analyses of political figures like Zacchaeus in order to discern their self-interest (in both the worst and best senses of that phrase). To analyze someone's self-interest we ask the question: What makes them tick? How do they derive power and use it for themselves and for those to whom they are beholden—and what might change these dynamics, enabling them to see and understand that others are hurt by their exercise of power?

A power analysis of Zacchaeus surely would recognize that he is a Roman minion. But it would recognize also ways in which he is a pawn in the Roman system—caught in a bind as both an oppressor and as one who is himself oppressed.[10] In terms that I have been using, Zacchaeus is a both a crucifier and crucified. In Luke's story, he seems to be struggling with this tension, for in response to the kindness and grace that Jesus extends to him, he pledges generous commitment to reparations for his past misdeeds—well beyond what was required by Torah. He provides a snapshot of an enemy in process of becoming a friend. This proves yet again that there are no permanent enemies and no permanent friends—just persons in the process either of shutting down or awakening to God's salvation—awakening to their kinship with God and others.

At the close of Luke's story, Jesus publicly affirms of Zacchaeus, in the presence of grumblers, that "Today salvation has come to this house, because he too is a son of Abraham" (Luke 19:9)—which is to say, "he's one of us"—a member of God's family, God's covenant people. Jesus restores him to community, emphasizing that he is kin. Thus notions of kindness and kinship flow from this story and they do so on account of Christ—our kin, our kind—who calls us to see our kin and our kind in everyone and everything, and to respond to everyone and everything—even our enemies—with God's own loving kindness or *hesed* and mercy.

---

10. See Boesak and DeYoung, *Radical Reconciliation*, 73.

Something as basic as our breath can play a role in keeping kindness and kinship at the forefront of our awareness. The "cruciform" or cross-shaped breath prayer can enable us to live more deeply into this expression of the Spirit's fruit and power in our lives, for it entails breathing in the Spirit of God that brings resurrection and life amid the death-tending stuff of our lives, and breathing out all that keeps us from loving God and from being kind (or kin) to others, to ourselves, and to the whole creation. The breath prayer is something you can practice for an extended period and at any and every moment of the day.

I invite you now to pray the Cruciform Breath Prayer with special attention to how God's Spirit might be calling you and your faith community to embody the political virtue of kindness—your compassionate interconnections with everyone (including your enemies) and everything. Then, stay with this awareness throughout the activities of your day, conscious of your interconnections with God, with everyone, and with all creation, compassionately and nonviolently resisting and transforming all that deforms life.

9

Generosity or Doing Good: The Sixth Political Fruit of the Spirit

WHEN I PONDER THE fruit of generosity or doing good (*agathōsynē* in Greek), the parable of the Good Samaritan (Luke 10:25–37) comes to mind, and the reason is the manner in which Jesus depicts him. Jesus describes the Samaritan's approach to a man who was robbed, beaten, and left near death by thieves in this way: "But a Samaritan while traveling came near him; and when he *saw* him, he was *moved* with pity. He *went* to him and bandaged his wounds, having poured oil and wine on them. Then he put him on his own animal, brought him to an inn, and took care of him" (Luke 10:33–34, emphasis added). Notice the verbs that describe the Samaritan's response: he "saw," "was moved," and "went"—verbs which correspond to three dimensions of the whole self (mind, heart, and will) delineated in the Great Commandment: "you shall love the Lord your God with all your *heart*, and with all your soul, and with all your *mind*, and with all your *strength*. . . . You shall love your neighbor as yourself" (Mark 12:28–31). Indeed, Luke's version of the Great Commandment and Jesus' endorsement of it (Luke 10:25–28) set the stage for the parable of the Good Samaritan (Luke 10:29–37), which Jesus narrates in response to a lawyer's question: "who is my neighbor?"

New Testament scholar Amy-Jill Levine's pointed and insightful commentary on the lawyer's query is quite striking. See what you think:

> For our parable, the lawyer's question is . . . misguided. To ask "Who is my neighbor" is a polite way of asking, "Who is not my neighbor?" or "Who does not deserve my love?" or "Whose lack of food or shelter can I ignore?" or "Whom I can hate?" The answer Jesus gives is, "No one." Everyone deserves that love—local or alien, Jews or gentile, terrorist or rapist, everyone.[1]

Levine goes on to argue that Jesus regards the Samaritan, an enemy of the Jews, as a neighbor deserving of love—a neighbor who was generous with the man set upon by thieves.

Interestingly, in Mark Allan Powell's discussion of the virtue of "generosity" in the New Testament he, too, highlights this emphasis on enemies as neighbors deserving of our love—as well as the parable of the Good Samaritan:

> Christian teaching . . . has extolled generosity to strangers and/or enemies. Jesus indicated that there is nothing special about people who do good to their own kind (Luke 6:33); his followers were to be known as people who give to everyone and do good to all, even those who hate them (Matt 5:42–48; Luke 6:30–36). Jesus' parable of the good Samaritan illustrates precisely this point: those who understand what Jesus means by "love your neighbor" will open their purses and use their money generously to meet the needs of people who do not affirm or even respect their religion (Luke 10: 33–35).[2]

There is, of course, much more to this parable about generosity than the opening of a wallet. The overcoming of binary oppositions of "us versus them" is also clearly on display. In fact, at the conclusion of the parable, Jesus flips the question he was asked ("Who is my neighbor?"), inviting the lawyer's response to a very different one: "Which of these do you think *was* a neighbor to the man who fell into the hands of the robbers?" It appears that from Jesus' perspective, the important question is not "who *is* my neighbor," but rather "how can I *be* a neighbor?" In his response

1. Levine, *Short Stories by Jesus,* 93.
2. Powell, "Generosity," 324.

to Jesus' question, the lawyer cannot even bear to say "*the Sa-maritan.*" Choking on the identity of the "other," he obfuscates, admitting, "*The one* who showed him mercy." Others "saw" the wounded man but were not moved to action. But the Samaritan saw, was moved to compassion, and acted upon it, conveying Luke's emphasis on the fact that if we love God fully with all of who we are, we will be moved to loving, active generosity that benefits those whom God loves, for human generosity, in biblical perspective, is grounded in God's own generosity. It is a fruit of God's own Spirit, as the epistle of James notes: "every generous act of giving" comes from God (James 1:17).[3] The fact that a de-spised Samaritan embodies this kind of generous giving makes Jesus' parable all the more impressive—and evidently, harder for his interlocutor to swallow. The Samaritan, an enemy, embodies divine generosity when he extends himself in love and empathy, acting on behalf of the well-being of a vulnerable other. Lest we let ourselves off the hook (as readers who may not harbor hostil-ity toward Samaritans), Amy-Jill Levine concludes her own com-mentary on the parable with challenging questions of her own:

> Can we finally agree that it is better to acknowledge the humanity and the potential to do good in the enemy, rather than to choose death? Will we be able to care for our enemies, who are also our neighbors? Will we be able to bind up their wounds rather than blow up their cities? And can we imagine that they might do the same for us? Can we put into practice that inaugura-tion promise of not leaving the wounded traveler on the road? The biblical text—and concern for humanity's future—tell us we must.[4]

Generosity may require placing our resources in service of another in need; but it also requires more: overcoming combative opposition to the other. This, in fact, is a key to unlocking Paul's letter to the Galatians in Brigitte Kahl's reading of it. As she ex-plains, "Paul boldly declares that he is crucified to the (old) *kosmos*

3. Powell, "Generosity," 324.
4. Levine, *Short Stories by Jesus*, 117.

and the *kosmos* to him, because the dichotomies on which the established world order (*kosmos*) rests (like the antithesis of circumcision/Jews versus foreskin/gentiles) have been dissolved and left behind. . . . Paul is crucified to the entire *kosmos* with its multiple polarities, not just its faith-based, ethnic, and social divisions."[5] Kahl underlines the fact that in Galatians 5–6, Paul uses the Greek word *allēlōn* ("one another," which stems from *allos-allos*—literally "other-other") no less than seven times: e.g., "through love becomes slaves *to one another*" (5:13); "If you bite and devour *one another*, take care that you are not consumed by *one another*" (5:15); "Let us not become conceited, competing against *one another*, envying *one another*" (5:26). This could best be translated as "one-and-otherness," suggesting a mystical union between one and the other in Christ.[6]

I find it significant that in these same chapters, Paul's juxtaposition of the crucifying "works of the flesh" with the life-giving "fruit of the Spirit" follows directly on the heels of his own declaration that the whole of the law is summed up by the commandment to "love your neighbor as yourself" (Gal 5:14). So on this account, the Spirit-empowered fruit of generosity entails loving one's neighbors and acting on behalf of their well-being, no matter what their identity, because in Christ all such polarizing divisions are erased, and the baptized community that embodies this kind of generosity represents the beachhead of God's new creation.

Visible signs of communal generosity are integral features of Christian worship and part of its witness. One such sign, simple though it may seem, is the "passing of the peace," which in my own tradition usually follows corporate confession of sin: "Since God has forgiven us in Christ, let us forgive one another. Greet one another with the peace of Christ." Luke Bretherton contends that this sharing of a sign of peace (whether a kiss or a handshake) in Christian worship contains the potential to constitute an alternative social order in Christ that overcomes enmity. The sign of peace is a conciliatory gesture that "recognizes the reality of ongoing

5. Kahl, "Galatians," 522.
6. Kahl, *Galatians Re-Imagined*, 269.

divisions and unjust inequalities and thence the need to become enemies reconciled.[7] The transformation of divisions and inequalities involves healing, exorcism/deliverance (which can entail abolition of systemically evil practices and institutions), and the formation of new, eschatologically anticipative ways of being alive with and for others."[8] In other words, the sharing of a sign of peace in worship pointedly raises the question, how can I be a neighbor?—a question that engages our vision, emotions, and actions on behalf of others, particularly those in need. This liturgical moment provides a very tactile, concrete sign of generosity.

The Eucharist, or Lord's Supper, contains similar signs and gestures of generous hospitality. According to theologian Gordon Lathrop, the Eucharist is a "broken symbol." What he means by this is that while the meal is made up of elements that we commonly recognize in our culture—such as bread, cup, the setting of the table—during Eucharist this common material is criticized, reoriented, and sifted.[9] The Eucharist thus stands in marked contrast to an "invitation only" meal where an RSVP is expected within a reasonable time frame, where the guests bring a suitable gift, where place cards are used to designate seats—presumably near someone with whom we feel comfortable or whose influence is sought.

By contrast, the eucharistic meal, while elegant in its own way, is also rude and ghastly in others. We use our hands (washed or not) for the bread and the cup, and we pass it to whoever is sitting next to us, or in line right behind us, whoever that person might be—friend, enemy, or perhaps someone who has spent the night on the street. As we share the bread and cup we say words that would seem horrible in any other setting, words like, "the body of Christ given for you," or "the blood of Christ shed for you"—but words that also hold the potential for healing and liberation in the crucified and risen Christ. The meal is a foretaste of the heavenly banquet, a foreshadowing of the kingdom of God, a remembrance of the manna in the wilderness where God supplies all our needs

7. Bretherton, *Christ and the Common Life*, 216
8. Bretherton, *Christ and the Common Life*, 220.
9. Lathrop, *Holy People*, 194.

and prefigures the unconditional, unearned grace that can only be received as a gift whereby we learn to receive one another as gifts. The meal, in sum, teaches us generosity, a political fruit of the Spirit that shapes us to be neighbors, to receive others as neighbors, and to embody gestures of new creation.

I invite you to pray the Cross Examen or the Cruciform Breath Prayer with special attention to how God's Spirit might be calling you and your faith community to embody the political virtue of generosity. As you pray, ponder not only the lawyer's question ("Who is my neighbor?"), but also Jesus' question ("How can I be a neighbor?"). Reflect on the fact that generosity opens not only our wallets, but also our hearts; it expands our vision and moves us to actions on behalf of others. Then, as in the Cross Examen or the Cruciform Breath Prayer, stay with this awareness throughout the activities of your day, conscious of your interconnections with God, with everyone, and with everything, compassionately and nonviolently resisting and transforming all that deforms human life and all creation.

10

Faithfulness: The Seventh Political Fruit of the Spirit

> But the scripture has imprisoned all things under the power of sin, so that what was promised through faith in Jesus Christ might be given to those who believe. Now before faith came, we were imprisoned and guarded under the law until faith would be revealed. Therefore the law was our disciplinarian until Christ came, so that we might be justified by faith. (Gal 3:22–24)

ONE OF THE MOST intriguing debates in recent Pauline scholarship bears on an understanding of the seventh fruit of the Spirit: faithfulness. The debate hinges on a translation question with significant theological implications: Are we justified by grace through "faith *in* Christ" or by "the faith/faithfulness *of* Christ" (e.g., Gal 2:15–21)? The Greek phrase in question (*pistis tou Christou*) can be translated either way (as what grammarians term an "objective genitive" or a "subjective genitive"). For centuries, the former translation option was in vogue. Indeed, a watchword of the sixteenth-century Protestant Reformation was that justification is by grace through faith [*in* Christ] apart from works of the law. We are saved not by works—by what we do, but by our faith *in* Jesus Christ. Christ, in other words, is the "object" of faith. In more recent decades, compelling arguments have been made for the latter option, which takes Christ as the subject, rather than object, of faith: we are justified by *Christ's* own faithfulness. *Jesus'* faithfulness, that is, the trust in God he exhibited in his own life and death, is the source of our salvation, rather than our own cognitive disposition or confessional orthodoxy. Those who favor the latter option (which increasingly represents the majority scholarly opinion) maintain that by the power of God's Spirit we are incorporated into the faithfulness of Christ. This, of course, has implications for our own lives of faithfulness, for just as Christ proclaimed the kingdom (the politics of God), embodied it in his life, confronted all that deformed and defaced God's good creation, and suffered the consequences, so do those who follow him, for the Spirit empowers us for lives of faithfulness in the world resembling his own. As biblical scholar Richard Hays explains:

> In a mysterious way, Jesus has enacted our destiny, and those who are in Christ are shaped by the pattern of his self-giving death. He is the prototype of redeemed humanity. Thus for Paul, "the faithfulness of Jesus Christ" has an incorporative character. That is why Paul says, "I have been crucified with Christ, and it is no longer I who live, but it is Christ who lives in me. And the life I now live in the flesh I live by the faithfulness of the Son of God, who loved me and gave himself for me" (Gal 2:19–20). *Jesus is not merely a good moral example; rather, his story transforms and absorbs the world. The old world has been crucified and new creation has broken in through Jesus' death and resurrection* (Gal 6:14–15).[1]

The debated translation options are not necessarily mutually exclusive. Bruce Longenecker, for example, holds together the implications of both translations (faith in Christ and the faith/faithfulness of Christ) in a compelling way:

> Whereas Paul can speak of being crucified with the crucified one, of dying with the one who died in order to live with the one who lives . . . so he can talk of Christian participation in the faithfulness (πίστις) of Jesus through their own faith (πίστις)—a faith occasioned and inspired by the coming of Christ's faithfulness. If God's in-breaking into the world has emerged from the faithfulness of Christ and resulted in the establishment of a new world, so Christian faith in the Faithful One is the means of

1. Hays, *The Faith of Christ*, xxxi (emphasis mine).

participation in that eschatological event, in anticipation of its future culmination.[2]

These new perspectives on Paul also inform a more expansive understanding of the theological concept of "justification." The Greek word for "justification" (*dikaiosynē*) can also be translated as "righteousness" and as "justice." In fact, Pauline scholar Michael Gorman suggests that whenever we see the word "justification" or "righteousness" in Paul's writings, restorative justice is in view, because the original word carries this meaning. Indeed, Gorman claims that for Paul the whole goal of human existence is to participate in the cruciform, justice-seeking faithfulness of God in Christ. God's Spirit is forming us for such a life. Thus, Gorman notes that his thought-provoking book *Becoming the Gospel* could well have been entitled "Becoming the Justice of God," for "Paul's gospel is the announcement of the arrival and power of God's right-wising, transformative justice in Jesus Christ.... To put it simply: the cross of Christ reveals a missional, justifying, justice-making God and creates a missional, justified, justice-making people."[3]

Putting all this together, what does "faithfulness" as a fruit of the Spirit entail? Stated simply, what it means is that the Spirit incorporates us—individually and corporately—into the faithfulness of the justice-seeking God in Christ. It means that by the power of the Spirit in our midst, the life that Jesus embodied is taking shape in our own lives. So what will lives that exhibit the fruit of faithfulness look like? The shape of Jesus' own life provides the clues. Just as Jesus proclaimed the coming of God's politics of reconciling, restorative justice and love, we too are being formed for such proclamation. And as God's Spirit forms in us the same faithfulness that was in Jesus, then like him we too will confront all that deforms and defaces God's good creation, because such things mimic the power that crucified Jesus, and God in Christ is bringing resurrection and life out of cruciform places, large and small. Thus faithfulness surely entails standing with the

2. Longnecker, *The Triumph*, 106.
3. Gorman, *Becoming the Gospel*, 8.

abandoned, the forsaken, and the deserted, because God in Christ knows what it is to be forsaken. It prompts us to seek reconciliation with others with whom there is any enmity, because God in Christ reconciled enemies. It prompts us to bring all of our resources to bear on God's justice-seeking, reconciling, forgiving, restoring work. It inspires commitment to practices of the faith such as prayer and worship, for Jesus himself was faithful in such things, in order that we, too, may be attuned to the movement of the Spirit and discern those places where God's rule—God's politics—is struggling toward realization now.

Lives of faithfulness exhibit no divide between private and public realms, for embodying the way of Christ bears on all aspects of our lives, including our work, our vocations, and our avocations. And when national politics seem hopelessly polarized, spawning demonizing stereotypes, faithfulness prompts us to seek common ground with those whose politics are not our own—to extend a hand across the aisle, because God in Christ was faithful in extending himself to others held in contempt, like Zacchaeus, a despised tax collector and Roman stooge, on the assumption that no one is fated and transformation can happen in unlikely places.

Faithfulness surely means being there for children, because Jesus was faithful in welcoming and embracing children who were among the lowest of the low, to be seen and not heard. It means welcoming the immigrant and refugee, because Jesus embraced the stranger. It means embracing conversation with those whose race, gender, class, or sexual orientation is not our own, because as the Apostle Paul claims, the faithfulness of Jesus into which we are baptized washes away violence, both spiritual and physical, between Greek and Jew, slave and free, male and female. And it means doing justice, loving mercy, and walking humbly with God, because that is what Jesus' own life of faithfulness displayed.

Most importantly, it means incorporation into the faithfulness of Jesus in the quotidian, the minutiae of daily life. As noted in chapter 1, when Jesus instructs his followers that discipleship involves taking up "their cross" (Matt 16:24; Mark 8:34; Luke 9:23) he was not suggesting that they pick up a cross they did not already bear, but rather that they acknowledge and name the crosses of oppression in their own lives and those around them, and resist all such savage forces. In other words, crucifixion was (and is) a daily occurrence. Indeed, Luke's version of this teaching acknowledges the quotidian nature of crucifixion, for Jesus instructs disciples to "take up their cross *daily*" (Luke 9:23). Interestingly, theologian Ada María Isasi-Díaz contends that attention to the quotidian is a necessary feature of grassroots life for the Latinx community. She speaks of the daily struggle to survive and to live fully, resisting forces that diminish life at every moment of the day:

> What we must insist on are small structural changes, changes that will make a difference someday precisely because they take into consideration the personal, the specific, the local. We are bent on changes that set processes in motion and do not seek "true solutions" because these seem to ignore particularity, diversity and difference. Our struggles give priority to what is needful and useful, to effectiveness on a small scale, at the level of everyday reality. We give priority to creating relationship instead of insisting on changing bureaucratic set ups that will continue to ignore the personal. . . . *Mujerista* theology adovocates and tries to live an on-going process of conversion that focuses on the need to bring radical change in those everyday, violent, and exploitative practices that oppress and marginalize us.[4]

Isasi-Díaz's poignant reflection calls to mind a Gospel story in which we see Jesus' own uncanny attunement to the personal, the specific, the local on full display—his close attention to the quotidian struggle and need with which a sidelined beggar named Bartimaeus contends (Mark 10:46–52). It is one of my favorite stories to use when introducing the ancient contemplative practice of praying with Scripture attributed to St. Ignatius of Loyola (1491–1556, founder of the Jesuit religious order) and canonized in his Spiritual Exercises. The Ignatian method of contemplation invites us to use our imaginations as a source of prayerful understanding as we

4. Isasi-Díaz, *La Lucha Continues*, 2–3.

engage Scripture. Thus as we pray with a Gospel story like that of Bartimaeus, we are invited to visualize the scene and imagine ourselves as participants in it—even to contemporize the scene in our own time, place, and locality—our own quotidian reality. One begins simply by reading the story slowly, and asking questions such as the following: Where am I in this story, and with whom do I identify? What strikes me about the setting, and how does it intersect with my own life context? I invite you to read Mark 10:46–52 with these questions in mind:

> They came to Jericho. As he and his disciples and a large crowd were leaving Jericho, Bartimaeus son of Timaeus, a blind beggar, was sitting by the roadside. When he heard that it was Jesus of Nazareth, he began to shout out and say, "Jesus, Son of David, have mercy on me!" Many sternly ordered him to be quiet, but he cried out even more loudly, "Son of David, have mercy on me!" Jesus stood still and said, "Call him here." And they called the blind man, saying to him, "Take heart; get up, he is calling you." So throwing off his cloak, he sprang up and came to Jesus. Then Jesus said to him, "What do you want me to do for you?" The blind man said to him, "My teacher, let me see again." Jesus said to him, "Go; your faith has made you well." Immediately he regained his sight and followed him on the way.

So where are you in this story, and with whom do you identify? What strikes you about the setting and resonates with your own?

Perhaps a few observations about the story might prompt reflection. One of the interesting things about this story is the explicit naming of the blind man and his status: "Bartimaeus son of Timaeus, a blind beggar." In Aramaic, the name Bartimaeus actually means "son of Timaeus"; so what are we to make of the fact that the name is referenced twice? Is this unnecessary redundancy, or is the story making an emphatic point? This is the only story in Mark in which the recipient of a healing is named, which would suggest that the name itself is significant and demands attention. Theologian Gordon Lathrop's commentary on this point is thought-provoking: the name Timaeus is Greek, not Jewish, and this particular name was widely associated with one of the most influential philosophical books in the ancient world—Plato's *Timaeus*—which set out the order of the cosmos and humankind in it. Lathrop makes a compelling case that in Plato's work, the blind are considered "incapable of being the kind of philosopher Timaeus envisions, incapable of attaining the good life, not able to follow the divine courses of the sky"[5]—incapable, in other words, of taking a place among the elite, the privileged, the upper crust. So, on this account, could the story of the blind beggar named Bartimaeus son of Timaeus represent a deliberate reversal of Plato's worldview?[6] In it, one who was down and out, deemed incapable of the good life, finds his sight restored and follows Jesus on the divine way.

The story also bears witness to the faithfulness and attentiveness of Jesus in the midst of quotidian reality. The crowd sternly tried to silence the blind beggar who called out to Jesus, repeatedly, for mercy; but Jesus "stood still," registered the cry, and insisted on attending to him. The crowd quickly changed its tune ("Take heart; get up, he is calling you") and brought the blind beggar into his presence for healing. The story suggests that those who, like Bartimaeus, follow Jesus "on the way," will attune their own ears to cries of suffering in their own quotidian contexts. In so doing, they may redirect the attention of others as well, for as Kathy Black points out, sometimes it only takes the example of one person in leadership, who honors those considered expendable in society, to turn a crowd![7]

I invite you to attend to this story, reflecting on your own capacity to hear the cries of those by the roadside—the sidelined, the overlooked, the marginalized, the expendable. Are there ways in which I ignore or even silence such persons, and how might the insistent faithfulness of Jesus redirect my attention to their need? Can I embody his faithfulness in my own life with concrete acts

5. Lathrop, *Holy Ground,* 29.

6. Lathrop, *Holy Ground,* 31.

7. Black, *A Healing Homiletic,* 82.

of compassion and restoration? As you reflect on this story, where else does your imagination lead you?

As you contemplate the story of Bartimaeus, I invite you to also pray the Cross Examen or the Cruciform Breath Prayer with special attention to how God's Spirit might be calling you and your faith community to embody the political virtue of faithfulness. As you pray, ponder deeply how the Spirit of God might be forming in you the faithfulness of the crucified and risen Christ—in the midst of quotidian reality, the daily minutiae of your life and work. Then, as in the Cross Examen or the Cruciform Breath Prayer, stay with this awareness throughout your activities during this day, conscious of your interconnections with God, with everyone, and with everything, compassionately and nonviolently resisting and transforming all that deforms human life and all creation.

11

Gentleness: The Eighth Political Fruit of the Spirit

MANY REGARD THE APOSTLE Paul as the most enigmatic figure of Christian history. Depending on who you talk to, Paul can be viewed as sexist, homophobic, pro-slavery, or anti-Jewish, and associated with a range of other unflattering attitudes, behaviors, and defects. Alas, these are misunderstandings of Paul based on a questionable history of interpretation that fails to attend closely to Paul's authentic writings (that is, letters that can be attributed to his direct authorship) and nuances of them. I hope I have managed to deconstruct a few questionable stereotypes about the man in the course of this study.

However, there is one bad behavior that the apostle himself readily admits to: his own life of violence against the early Jesus movement. Prior to his conversion, he persecuted early Christians—and mourns this recollection. Why did he do so? We do not know for sure, though it is usually attributed to some form of religious zealotry. Some suspect he could not wrap his head around what might have seemed to be a blasphemous notion: a crucified Jewish Messiah. Whatever the case may be, after his conversion Paul turned away from a violent way of life—an important dimension of his life that has only recently begun to garner attention. During his "Damascus road experience," Paul heard a voice, identified as that of the risen Christ, saying to him, "Saul, Saul, why are you persecuting me?" (Acts 9:4). Encounter with the crucified and risen Lord thus entailed for him an unmasking of violence and of all powers that participate in it—especially in the ultimate expression of it, a Roman cross.

Paul came to the realization that the crucified Jesus was raised by God and alive in the lives of his followers; thus, to perpetuate hostility and violence against Christ's followers was to crucify Christ all over again. In fact, in his Letter to the Galatians, Paul claims that the world, with its hostility, has been crucified to him, and he to the world. It has been washed away in his baptism into the life, death, and resurrection of Jesus (Gal 6:14). Thus, the very premise for his letter to the churches of the Roman province of Galatia was to point out what should have been obvious to them—that any accommodation to violence is a betrayal of the God who suffers and seeks justice and reconciliation in a crucified world.

This brings us to the next-to-last fruit of the Spirit in Galatians 5: gentleness. This fruit takes us into the belly of the beast, for it bears on our understanding of power—how it is used in the world, and how we ourselves use it to influence the thinking, feeling, and acting of others. Power can be exercised in one of two ways: either as "power over" or "power with." At the risk of oversimplification, "power over" tends toward potentially crucifying uses of power in the world. As an old adage conveys, "If you've got a hammer in your hand, everything (and everyone) looks like a nail." Much of our experience of "politics" at work in our world is based on the "power over" model—the power of domination (whether subtle or overt) that aims to bend and subjugate the hearts, minds, and wills of others. In his book *Jesus and the Disenfranchised*, Howard Thurman, the prominent African American philosopher, theologian, educator, and civil rights leader, tells a story about a dog that lived in his neighborhood when he was a child—a story that that captures the deforming impact of percussive politics:

> There was a dog that lived at the end of my street in my hometown. Every afternoon, he came down the street by the house. I could always hear him coming, giving a quick, sharp yelp in front of certain yards along the way. He was not hit by flying stones; each boy would catch the dog's eye and draw his arm back—the yelp followed

> immediately. The threat was sufficient to secure the re-
> action because, somewhere in the past, that particular
> motion had been identified with pain and injury. Such
> is the role of the threat of violence. It is rooted in a past
> experience, actual or reported, which tends to guarantee
> the present reaction of fear. . . . There are few things more
> devastating than to have it burned into you that you do
> not count and that no provisions are made for the literal
> protection of your person.[1]

Thurman's story speaks to the critical importance of listening to
the knowledge that emerges from those intimately acquainted
with the reality of oppressive violence. Some refer to such knowledge as "privileged," i.e., essential, because it provides the best
"read on what is really going on."[2] In a similar vein, theologian
Vincent Lloyd has coined the concept of "black natural law" that
reflects on human nature from the standpoint of oppression. Such
a perspective exposes the idolatry of political structures that favor
the "interest of the few." Indeed, Lloyd maintains that black natural
law builds relationship and power from the grassroots that resists
the presumed wisdom and power of the privileged. It interrogates
and challenges human laws that deform and deface human digni-
ty.[3] It seems to me that black natural law is very much akin to the
political theology of the cross—what we can call "cruciform wisdom." To paraphrase Martin Luther, such a theology or wisdom
never ignores or condones structures of oppression; instead, the
theology of the cross calls it what it is.

Paul's own life attested that cruciform wisdom can have redemptive power in the lives of the privileged. In his case, it transformed a zealous persecutor into a nonviolent apostle. Moreover,
as we have seen, Jesus himself stood with the oppressed, listened
to their cries and resisted forces that disfigured their lives; indeed,
because this characterized his life and ministry, he himself was
crucified. Thus we privilege knowledge stemming from Jesus' life

---

1. Thurman, *Jesus and the Disinherited*, 29.

2. Bretherton, *Christ and the Common Life*, 305

3. Lloyd, *Black Natural Law*, ix–xi, 117.

and ministry. He embodied cruciform wisdom—wisdom that comes from standing in solidarity with the oppressed. In fact, in 1 Corinthians 1:18–2:16, Paul speaks explicitly, eloquently, and paradoxically of the crucified and risen Christ as the very wisdom and power of God, countering status quo and imperial notions of wisdom and power. Contemplation of Christ's sufferings—of the cross as the wisdom and power (and thus the very revelation) of God—"disrupts and reconfigures" what we see and do.[4]

If I understand Paul's conversion experience, his encounter with the crucified and risen Christ began just such a process in his own life; one of transforming, healing, and liberating the hold on him of the dominating, fear-based percussive politics of his world. It disrupted and reconfigured his vision and practice. Jesus Christ, after all, was mortally wounded by the percussive politics of Caesar, and his wounds exposed what was really going on in the world—which is why Paul claims that he bears in his body the marks (the "stigmata") of Jesus. As we embody Christ (as believers who are "in Christ"), we begin to see how the politics of the world wounds all of us. We also hear the divine call to be in solidarity with the wounded. Indeed, Paul's conversion, according to Davina Lopez, brings about a completely different personal, social, and political self-consciousness. She makes this poignant observation about Paul's presentation of himself after his conversion:

> Paul models a defeated, and not heroic, male body. His defeated body is identified with slavery and with Christ, who is in him and crucified alongside him. . . . Paul goes down to the bottom position within a vertical hierarchical arrangement. . . . Paul identifies himself as dead, defeated, and weak on the underside of a world-wide power structure. Instead of ravaging and persecuting, Paul performs as a man for and with, and not against and above, others . . . There is nothing extraordinarily warrior-like or heroic about Paul's defeated, penetrated male body: it is a body reminiscent of numerous casualties of Roman encounters with barbarian nations. It bears the "marks of Christ" (Gal 6:17), again, the marks of capital

---

4. Bretherton, *Christ and the Common Life*, 68.

punishment. . . . Paul's consciousness concerning his
marginalization enables him to go down and stand in a
line with all the defeated nations. Standing in line with
the defeated nations means that he has "become like
them" (Gal 4:13).[5]

As we have noted, Paul gives the most pointed expression
to his new sense of self in Galatians 2:19–20, when he insists, "I
have been crucified with Christ; and it is no longer I who live, but
Christ who lives in me." To be co-crucified and co-risen in Christ
is not only to live in solidarity with the excluded, the vanquished,
the rejected, and the outsider—that is, with all who have experienced crucifixion—it is also to confess our own participation
in all such crucifixions. To make such a radical confession and
to stand in solidarity with all who experience crucifixion is to
relinquish power of any dominating sort—"power over," and to
live into a very different kind of power—"power with," or what we
might call "gentle" power.

Political theorist Hannah Arendt defined power as the "ability not just to act but to act in concert."[6] It is especially, for Paul,
the ability to act in concert with the wounded of the earth. For it
is only at the very places of woundedness that we are healed, liberated, redeemed, and transformed into a people who embody the
faithfulness of Jesus in our world and live into the power of resurrection life, thereby serving as a beachhead of God's new creation.
In short, forming in us the mind of Jesus—his life, death, and
resurrection—is the key to the fruit of the Spirit (and the political
virtue) Paul names as "gentleness."

When we look at Jesus' life, in scenes conveyed by the Gospels, we see the virtue of gentleness on prominent display, perhaps
nowhere more so than in his attitude toward children, who bore
little status in the ancient world. To illustrate this point, biblical
scholar John Crossan tells the chilling story of a letter sent by a
first-century Egyptian man to his pregnant wife, who was obvi-
ously living at some distance from him. In the letter, he gave her

5. Lopez, *Apostle to the Conquered*, 138–39.
6. Quoted in Crosby, *The Fruit*, 239.

instructions to be followed at the time of birth: "If it's a boy," he says, "let it be; if it's a girl, cast it out."[7] This counsel strikes us as shocking, but it was not unusual in the ancient world where "exposure" of unwanted infants was a widespread practice. Indeed, Crossan uses this story to illumine with stark clarity the vulnerable status of an infant child in the Mediterranean world.

He then juxtaposes the terror of this letter to the story of Jesus in Mark 10:13–16, in which he receives children in his midst: "Notice the framing words; touch, took in his arms, blessed, laid hands on."[8] These are words of a parent accepting a child into a family rather than casting it out. Crossan speculates that there must have been debate in Mark's community as to the status of abandoned children—whether to accept them into the community or not. In this story, the Markan Jesus provides a definitive answer to this question: as Crossan puts it, the kingdom of God is "a Kingdom of Children—a Kingdom of Nobodies."[9]

We experience and extend the gentle power of Jesus' touch and blessing in baptism and communion. That gentleness is the very foundation of our work in the world—integral to our vocations and avocations. In all the arenas of our lives, it entails the power of nonviolent, resistant love, exercised not as "power over," but as "power with." The gentle power of solidarity with the excluded, the vanquished, the rejected, the outsider, and the godforsaken is the essence of the political life of the followers of Jesus Christ in the world.

I invite you to pray the Cross Examen or the Cruciform Breath Prayer with special attention to how God's Spirit might be calling you and your faith community to embody the political virtue of gentleness. As you pray, ponder deeply and name the effects of "power over"—the crucifying effects of violence (both spiritual and physical) in your own life as well as in the lives of others around you. Ponder also what "power with" others might look like—and how God's Spirit might be forming in you the

7. Crossan, *Jesus*, 63–64.

8. Crossan, *Jesus*, 64.

9. Crossan, *Jesus*, 64.

political virtue of gentleness, especially as it is expressed toward the most vulnerable persons in the world around you. Then, as in the Cross Examen or the Cruciform Breath Prayer, stay with this awareness throughout the activities of your day, conscious of your interconnections with God, with everyone and with everything, compassionately and nonviolently resisting and transforming all that deforms human life and all of creation.

12

Self-Control: The Final Political Fruit of the Spirit

In his book *Good Citizens: Creating Enlightened Society*, Thich Nhat Hanh contends that the first ethical guideline of engaged spirituality is that "[w]e have to observe deeply what is happening around us before we can understand its causes and hope to transform it."[1] So what is happening around us? Consideration of the immediate American landscape, at least, suggests that all is not well. Among other things, we continue to endure the effects of a pulverizing, punishing political landscape in which Democrats and Republicans (and the nation as a whole) seem hopelessly polarized on immigration, health care, education, economics, and racial justice. It is hard to see a way forward. What is happening? Desperate immigrants and refugees continue to stream in our direction, to seek safe haven among us—some fleeing political persecution, ethnic conflict, and drug-related violence; others are desperate for the most basic of human necessities like food, shelter, education, and for jobs that no one else wants. All of them hope for a more promising, more secure future for their children—but they encounter increasingly harsh resistance, even cruel separation of children from their parents, at our borders and a rising tide of nativism.

What else is happening? Millions of Americans still do not have heath care. Homelessness and mass incarceration are still blights on our nation of epidemic proportion, and the environment

1. Hanh, *Good Citizens*, 15.

is in an ever-critical state of degradation. Moreover, the American dream still eludes the vast majority of our country's citizens, as the gap between the rich and the poor continues to widen. Indeed, our country is more divided than at any time in recent memory. Clearly, all is not well and there are no easy answers to the enormous challenges we face. The Apostle Paul's words in Romans 8 are as profoundly on target as when he first wrote them, when he observed that the whole creation and we ourselves are groaning for release, for salvation, to be set free from bondage (Rom 8:18–27).

We have to observe deeply what is happening around us before we can understand its causes and hope to transform it. And as you might anticipate, I contend that the theology of the cross, and in particular Paul's distinctive notion of it, is essential for Christian vision—for deep observation and discernment of what is happening around us. The cross exposes what is going on with singular clarity. Theologian Wendy Farley articulates this point profoundly:

> Christ's wounds show us what is going on all the time. Governments are murdering and torturing their people. There is affliction and despair. Illness and accident wrack our bodies; drought and pollution wrack the earth. Christ's wounds do not make these things go away. They show us where the Divine Eros [love] is in all of these things. Christ is there in the world, in hell, at the point of affliction's sword all the time, regardless of what anyone does, whether we pray or not, whether we hope or not. In prayer, in sickness, in death, Christ is "walking around our bedside." *Christ shows us Erotic power as the power that keeps the story moving toward freedom at every point*: at every creation, in beauty, in the dawning of understanding, in love between lovers, in the endless wanderings of the stars, in the first seed of erotic desire, in the dark night of souls, in death and in affliction, in the harrowing, in the release of captives.[2]

2. Farley, *The Wounding*, 145, emphasis added. By "erotic," Farley means the deep "desire" in us that reflects the image of God, as well as God's deep love for us and the whole creation.

The phrase in this poignant quote that most captures my attention is Farley's contention that the power of Christ is moving us towards "freedom at every point." This resonates profoundly with the central theme of Paul's letter to the Galatians: freedom as a central characteristic of the Christian life. The emphatic observations Paul makes in Gal 5:1 and 13 are pivotal ones: "For *freedom* Christ has set us free" (5:1) and "you were called to *freedom*, brothers and sisters" (5:13).

But it is critically important to unpack what that means, lest we misconstrue Paul on this point, because the freedom of which he speaks is not freedom of speech or choice or self-expression.[3] It is certainly not the unyoked, free-market, consumer freedom to do my own thing—the credo of modernity. The freedom of which Paul speaks is a divine gift, grounded in the liberating work of God in Jesus Christ. We are free because God in Christ has set us free, both *from* something and, at the same time, decidedly *for* something: we are set free from whatever binds us to live in the sphere of Christ's lordship, set free in the service of God, and thus set free to serve one another in love, for love is the proper exercise of freedom.[4]

Indeed, Paul paradoxically affirms that the exercise of freedom entails mutual service: "For you were called to freedom, brothers and sisters; only don't let this freedom be an opportunity to indulge your selfish impulses, but serve one another through love" (5:13 Common English Bible). Freedom, in other words, as Sam William has summarized it, "is not untrammeled personal autonomy. It is, rather, opportunity and possibility—the opportunity to love the neighbor without hindrance, the possibility of creating human communities based on mutual self-giving rather than the quest for power and status."[5]

Love, as you will recall, was the first fruit of the Spirit, and this backdrop brings us to the final one: self-control. This last fruit might seem to be the most pedestrian of all the aforementioned

3. Cousar, *Galatians*, 107–10.
4. Gench, "Galatians 5:1, 13–25," 291–92.
5. Williams, *Galatians*, 145.

ones, but it is vitally important, underlined by its position of importance as the final fruit in the list. Indeed, the bookends of the catalogue, love and self-control, frame and tie together all of the other fruit. Moreover, the fruit of self-control would not have gone unnoticed in the first-century context, for it was regarded as the chief virtue in the Greco-Roman world. The Stoic philosophers, for example, taught that while you might not be able to control anything else (e.g., your circumstances), you could always control your thoughts, and thus yourself.

But Paul's understanding of "self-control" is quite different than the Greco-Roman version of it. For one thing, it is not a virtue attained through knowledge and self-mastery, the focus of Greco-Roman ethics. Again, it is a divine gift grounded in the liberating work of God in Jesus Christ. Moreover, it is not an individual virtue but a communal one, a mark of the church—of a community that lives under the sway of the Spirit. If freedom, in Paul's view, entails both freedom *from* and freedom *for*, both love and self-control play crucial roles in facilitating the latter. Love, the first and foundational fruit of the Spirit, entails losing a false self in order to gain a more abundant self in, with, and for others and God's good creation; and self-control directs and disciplines the exercise of that love by tying or *tethering* us to cruciform love, to all the other fruit of the Spirit and, most especially, to others.

I like to think of the fruit of self-control in terms of the Spirit's "tethering" power. Freedom is not untrammeled personal autonomy, for self-control tethers our freedom to that of others. It takes us, so to speak, to the trenches of the world, and thus the trenches of ministry, where people are being crucified. The wounds of Christ expose the wounds of the world and our own woundedness; and the crucified and risen Christ shows us that it is among the wounded that God is at work, straining to bring life out of death. Paul urges those who have been baptized into the crucifixion and resurrection of Christ to "bear one another's burdens in order to fulfill the law of Christ" (Gal 6:2). The bearing of one another's burdens takes place in the trenches of death and life. And Paul contends that in those trenches, God's future is struggling toward realization now, taking shape in our lives and in the life of a strange new community that represents the beachhead of new creation—a community tethered to what really counts.

In the trenches, the crucified and risen Christ is tethering us to the immigrant facing deportation; to the homeless man or woman who cannot find a job because of a criminal record for which time has been served; to an inner-city high school student whose chances for a full and meaningful life are diminished because of substandard educational opportunities; and to our sisters and brothers across the globe in Asia, Central America, and Africa whose lives are adversely affected, politically and economically, by globalization.

The Spirit of the risen Christ is also tethering urban and rural churches together in a joint endeavor to stand shoulder to shoulder with the working poor; it tethers us to people of differing economic status and to people who do not vote like we do, whose sense of identity and worldview we frankly find difficult to understand; and it tethers us to one another in our own churches through thick and thin, in good times and bad. This tethering to the crucified and risen Christ, and thus to each other, marks points at which new creation and abundant life are emerging. Thus, as a cruciform virtue or fruit, self-control tethers us especially to broken places in our own lives and communities and in the life of the world.

Bryan Stevenson, a lawyer and social justice activist, has recently provided a stunning and inspiring vision of what it means to be tethered to the well-being of others in his highly acclaimed bestseller *Just Mercy: A Story of Justice and Redemption*. The volume shares the moving stories of incarcerated men, women, and children, many wrongly condemned, whom he has defended in his legal practice—a practice devoted to challenging bias against the poor and minorities trapped in our criminal justice system. But equally moving are the passages in which he reflects on the daunting challenges of his work and why he stays in it—disclosures such as this one near the end of the book that emerged on the night of the execution of Jimmy Dill at Holman prison in Alabama, a client he was not able to save from the death penalty.

As Stevenson wrestled with anger and exhaustion on that heartbreaking night, he found himself wondering, "Why do we want to kill all the broken people? What is wrong with us, that we think a thing like that can be right?"—questions which left him thinking, "It's time to stop. I can't do this anymore":

> For the first time I realized that my life was just full of brokenness. I worked in a broken system of justice. My clients were broken by mental illness, poverty, and racism. They were torn apart by disease, drugs and alcohol, pride, fear, and anger . . . In their broken state, they were judged and condemned by people whose commitment to fairness had been broken by cynicism, hopelessness, and prejudice. I looked at my computer and at the calendar on the wall. I looked again around my office at the stacks of files. I saw the list of our staff, which had grown to nearly forty people. And before I knew it, I was talking to myself aloud: "I can just leave. Why am I doing this?" It took me a while to sort it out, but I realized something sitting there while Jimmy Dill was being killed at Holman prison. After working for more than twenty-five years, *I understood that I don't do what I do because it's required or necessary or important. I don't do it because I have no choice. I do what I do because I'm broken, too.* My years of struggling against inequality, abusive power, poverty, oppression, and injustice had finally revealed something to me about myself. Being close to suffering, death, executions, and cruel punishments didn't just illuminate the brokenness of others; in a moment of anguish and heartbreak, it also exposed my own brokenness.[6]

Stevenson's eloquent insight resonates, I think, with Shelly Rambo's understanding of resurrection as confronting, rather than avoiding, our brokenness (explored in chapter 2). Rambo finds space for pondering our wounds in the room where the risen Christ appears to his disciples in John's gospel (John 20:19–29).

6. Stevenson, *Just Mercy*, 288 (emphasis mine).

John's account of this resurrection appearance is notable in that Jesus' hands and sides still bear the marks of crucifixion. Disciples are invited to see and touch those wounds, to attend to them, and in Rambo's view, this is the real power of the resurrection. She insists that because Jesus turns the disciples toward his wounds, we need to be doing the same, with a "readiness to hold pain and to stay with difficult truths" about the wounds that remain in our own lives. Rambo re-envisions "the meaning of resurrection, . . . locating its power in confronting, not erasing, the complexities of life beyond 'deaths,' whether literal or figurative."[7]

In terms that I have been using, the cruciform fruit of self-control can thus be described as tethering us, in the crucified and risen Christ, to broken places in our own lives and in the life of the world. It is a tethering wherein we experience resurrection in, with, and for others. It is a tethering in Christ that moves us toward freedom in, with, and for others. And in this tethering, the breath of the risen Christ gives us new possibilities of life amid our brokenness.

To return to the point with which we began: As we observe deeply what is happening around us, all is not well, and we may find ourselves fearful about directions in which our country and our world may be heading. As we attend to the wounds, we may find ourselves thinking, like Stevenson, "I can't do this anymore." But Christian existence is corporate in character, and what gives me hope are communities of faith which, by the power of God's Spirit at work within them, are countering the fear-mongering politics and broken realities of our day with cruciform love, joy, peace, patience, kindness, generosity, faithfulness, gentleness, and self-control. What gives me hope is confidence that, by the power of God's Spirit, we are tethered together in an all-pervasive love that will not let us go.

I invite you now to pray the Cross Examen or the Cruciform Breath Prayer with special attention to how God's Spirit is calling you and your faith community to embody the cruciform political virtue of *self-control* that tethers us to all the other fruit of the

7. Rambo, *Resurrecting Wounds*, 150.

Spirit and to others: the cruciform *love* that compels you to lose yourself in order to gain a fuller self in others; the cruciform *joy* of being caught up in something larger than yourself—in experiences of standing with the vulnerable, the oppressed or for a just cause; the cruciform *peace* to ponder deeply the enmities in your life and their crucifying effects, and how God might be bringing life and justice-seeking reconciliation amid divisions; the cruciform *patience* to contemplate deeply how hot anger can be changed into cold, patient anger—the kind of anger that stands with the oppressed and resists the crucifixions of the world; the cruciform *kindness* to be mindful of your kinship with everyone (including your enemies) and everything; the cruciform *generosity* to ponder not only the question "Who is my neighbor?," but also Jesus' question, "How can I be a neighbor?," questions that open not only our wallets, but also our hearts; the cruciform *faithfulness* to reflect deeply on how the Spirit of God might be forming the faithfulness of the crucified and risen Christ in your life and work; and the cruciform *gentleness* to consider the crucifying effects of "power over" politics, and what "power with" others might look like, especially as it is expressed toward the most vulnerable persons around you. As you pray, ponder how the Spirit of God in Christ might be tethering you to others in the trenches of your life and work and community. Then, as in the Cross Examen or the Cruciform Breath Prayer, stay with this awareness throughout the activities of your day, conscious of your interconnections with God, with everyone, and with everything, compassionately and nonviolently resisting and transforming all that deforms human life and all creation.

Epilogue

IN CLOSING, CONSIDER ONE last time Rachel Held Evans' incisive observation: "God is in the business of bringing dead things back to life.... [S]o if you want in on God's business, you better prepare to follow God to all the rock-bottom, scorched earth, dead-on-arrival corners of this world—including those in your own heart—because . . . that's where God gardens."[1] These words are, for me, a succinct summary of what we have explored in the preceding chapters—the deep and integral connection between contemplative practice and activism.

Throughout this book I have tried to demonstrate that both contemplative and activist Christian practices bear the same footprint of the Spirit of the crucified and risen Christ. Both are cruciform. The practice of cruciform contemplation creates space in which we discern the wounds—crucifixions—in our own lives and in our world and are given to understand the essential connection between the two. This impels, informs, and directs cruciform activism empowered by the political fruit of the Spirit. The political theology of the cross examined in this book thus has profound implications for our common life, for the marks of the cross interconnect us as we participate in God's own work of bringing life out of the death.

Recognizing these interconnections can profoundly galvanize, inform, and shape the way we engage in ministry. As the Spirit of the crucified and risen Christ forms in communities of disciples the mind of Jesus Christ and the political fruit of the

1. Evans, *Searching for Sunday*, 21.

119

Spirit, they become beachheads of new creation—outposts of the coming future as they embody resistance to crucifying powers and witness to the reconciliation that God has in mind for all. This is the work God has given us to do in the power of the Spirit. Godspeed in this witness and work!

Appendix

A Practicum on Engaged Spirituality

IN CHAPTER TWO, I noted the importance of using the Cross Examen and the Cruciform Breath Prayer in communal as well as personal contexts. The promise of transformation takes time and involves both personal and communal practice in a context where love, compassion, trust, and accountability are shared values—values rooted in the Spirit of the crucified and risen Christ. Individual practice of these disciplines is fairly self-explanatory; but you may be wondering what group practice of them might look like.

Thus, in this appendix, I provide an illustration that may be helpful—an example of how these practices informed and shaped the interaction of a small-group experience at my former church (The New York Avenue Presbyterian Church in Washington, DC) as we used the Cross Examen to great benefit, in ways that helped us reflect in depth together about the essential connection between contemplative practice and activism. I hope this story might provide food for thought as you imagine possibilities for communal practice in your own ministry setting.

In the fall of 2016, Theo Brown, the Director of our Scholar in Residence program, and I invited a group of ten people to make a year-long commitment to what came to be called "The Engaged Spirituality Group." The name of the group was suggested to us by a book entitled *Thomas Merton and Thich Nhat Hanh: Engaged Spirituality in an Age of Globalization*, by Robert King. In that book, King contends that Merton and Nhat Hanh "represent for me a new kind of spirituality that I believe may be the best hope for religious renewal in our day. . . . It is an engaged spirituality that combines traditional meditative practice with action directed at the eradication of the most intractable problems of contemporary life."[1] (Early on, King's book was an impetus for my own reflection on the topics that eventually found their way into the book you hold in your hands, *The Cross Examen*.) The group of ten included individuals who served on different boards of the church and played leadership roles in varied congregational ministries. Their common denominator was an expressed interest in both spirituality and activism.

Before our first meeting, the group was invited to read an early draft of chapter 1 of this book and to practice praying with the Cross Examen on a regular basis. At our first, exploratory meeting, we opened with group practice of the Cross Examen. This entailed a fifteen-minute guided meditation on the three stages of the Cross Examen, which I led with prompting questions such as those noted in chapter 1. Then we talked about our prayer experience (both individual experience with this practice in weeks leading up to the meeting, as well as our opening collective experience of it) and shared reflection that emerged from their engagement with the chapter I sent them in advance.

We talked about spirituality and activism as practices that share the same footprint and my contention that the spirituality of the cross can be a means of integrating the two endeavors. At the end of our conversation, participants were invited to ponder whether an engaged spirituality group was something for which they yearned and to which they were willing to make a commitment to meet together once a month. In advance of the next scheduled meeting, eight of the ten agreed to make the commitment. Theo and I also made this commitment.

For the next year, our group met once a month. Our commitment to each other between meetings was to daily practice of the Cross Examen (and the Cruciform Breath Prayer), to reflection on our common life and ministries in light of this prayer experience, and to keep a journal of insights that emerged. I asked them to practice at least ten to fifteen minutes a day, and

1. King, *Thomas Merton*, 1.

encouraged longer if time and interest allowed. I also sent them brief daily readings (via email)—short quotations from folk like Thich Nhat Hanh, Howard Thurman, and Dorothy Day, practitioners of engaged spirituality, to stimulate reflection—many of whom are quoted in this volume.

Our monthly meetings had a very simple agenda. We began with music—often a Taizé chant—and then spent about ten minutes in communal practice of the Cross Examen or the Cruciform Breath Prayer. Each participant then was invited to share, if so inclined, insights or reflection that emerged from their prayer practice during the last month (silence was always honored whenever participants were not moved to do so).

Occasionally, Theo Brown brought additional readings from folk who embodied engaged spirituality like Howard Thurman or Dorothy Day—readings that enriched our conversation. Each meeting concluded with more music and a period of prayer for each other. In the interim between meetings, we often conducted one-on-one meetings with each other in order offer more intimacy—small relational meetings that were also helpful in building community among us. Overall our work together helped deepen the connection between our spirituality and our ministry. Our time together was rich and often quite poignant and transformative, with ripple effects in both our individual lives and in our participation in varied ministries of the congregation!

Communal practice, of course, can take many forms. The experience I describe in this appendix is but one example. For other examples, or further description of the practice of group spirituality, I commend Rose Mary Dougherty's *Group Spiritual Direction: Community for Discernment* as a resource that can aid in utilizing the insights of this book.

Bibliography

"After Another Bloody Weekend in Chicago." https://www.pbs.org/newshour/show/another-bloody-weekend-violence-stricken-chicago.

Alexander, Michelle. *The New Jim Crow: Mass Incarceration in the Age of Colorblindness*. New York: The New Press, 2010.

Baker, Sharon. *Executing God: Rethinking Everything You've Been Taught about Salvation and the Cross*. Louisville: Westminster John Knox, 2013.

Bantum, Brian. *The Death of Race: Building a New Christianity in a Racial World*. Minneapolis: Fortress, 2016.

Black, Kathy. *A Healing Homiletic: Preaching and Disability*. Nashville: Abingdon, 1996.

Boesak, Allan, and Curtiss DeYoung. *Radical Reconciliation: Beyond Political Pietism and Christian Quietism*. Maryknoll, NY: Orbis, 2012.

Bolz-Weber, Nadia. *Pastrix: The Cranky, Beautiful Faith of a Sinner and Saint*. New York: Jericho, 2013.

Bretherton, Luke. *Christ and the Common Life: Political Theology and the Case for Democracy*. Grand Rapids: Eerdmans, 2019.

Brueggemann, Walter. "The Litany of Abundance, the Myth of Scarcity." *Christian Century*, March 24, 1999, 342.

Cone, James. *The Cross and the Lynching Tree*. Maryknoll, NY: Orbis, 2011.

Copeland, M. Shawn. *Knowing Christ Crucified: The Witness of African American Religious Experience*. Maryknoll, NY: Orbis, 2018.

Countryman, L. William. "Reconcile, Reconciliation." In *The Westminster Theological Wordbook of the Bible*, edited by Donald E. Gowan, 410–13. Louisville: Westminster, 2003.

Cousar, Charles B. *Galatians*. Interpretation. Atlanta: John Knox, 1982.

———. *The Letters of Paul*. Interpreting Biblical Texts. Nashville: Abingdon, 1996.

———. *Philippians and Philemon: A Commentary*. The New Testament Library. Louisville: Westminster John Knox, 2009.

Crosby, Michael. *The Fruit of the Spirit: Pauline Mysticism for the Church Today*. Maryknoll, NY: Orbis, 2015.

Crossan, John. *Jesus: A Revolutionary Biography*. New York: Harper Collins, 1994.

Culp, Kristine. *Vulnerability and Glory: A Theological Account.* Louisville: Westminster John Knox, 2010.

Davis, Ellen. "Land as Kin: Renewing the Imagination." In *Rooted and Grounded: Essays on Land and Christian Discipleship,* edited by Ryan D. Harker and Janeen Bertsche Johnson, 3–12. Eugene, OR: Pickwick, 2016.

Dougherty, Rose Mary. *Group Spiritual Direction: Community for Discernment.* Baltimore: School Sisters of Notre Dame, 1995.

Douglas, Kelly Brown. *Stand Your Ground: Black Bodies and the Justice of God.* Maryknoll, NY: Orbis, 2015.

Elliott, Neil. *The Arrogance of Nations: Reading Romans in the Shadow of Empire.* Minneapolis: Fortress, 2010.

———. *Liberating Paul: The Justice of God and the Politics of the Apostle.* Minneapolis: Fortress, 2006.

Evans, Rachel Held. *Searching for Sunday: Loving, Leaving, and Finding the Church.* Nashville: Thomas Nelson, 2018.

Farley, Wendy. *The Wounding and Healing of Desire: Weaving Heaven and Earth.* Louisville: Westminster John Knox, 2005.

Furnish, Victor Paul. *Theology and Ethics in Paul.* Nashville: Abingdon, 1968.

Gench, Frances Taylor. "Galatians 5:1, 13–25." *Interpretation* 46 (July 1992) 290–95.

Gorman, Michael J. *Becoming the Gospel: Paul, Participation, and Mission.* Grand Rapids: Eerdmans, 2015.

———. *Inhabiting the Cruciform God.* Grand Rapids: Eerdmans, 2009.

Graham, Larry Kent. *Moral Injury: Restoring Wounded Souls.* Nashville: Abingdon, 2017.

Hanh, Thich Nhat. *Breathe, You Are Alive: The Sutra on the Full Awareness of Breathing.* Berkeley: Parallax, 2008.

———. *Good Citizens: Creating Enlightened Society.* Berkeley, CA: Parallax, 2012.

———. *The Heart of Buddha's Teaching: Transforming Suffering into Peace, Joy and Liberation.* New York: Broadway, 1999.

———. *The Miracle of Mindfulness: An Introduction to the Practice of Mindfulness.* Boston: Beacon, 1975.

Harvey, Jennifer. *Dear White Christians: For Those Still Longing for Racial Reconciliation.* Grand Rapids: Eerdmans, 2014.

Hays, Richard. *The Faith of Christ: The Narrative Substructure of Galatians 3:1–4:11.* Grand Rapids: Eerdmans, 2002.

Hemingway, Ernest. *A Farewell to Arms.* New York: Charles Scribner and Sons, 1957.

Heschel, Abraham Joshua. *The Prophets.* Peabody, MA: Hendrickson, 1962.

Hooker, Morna. "Philippians." In *The New Interpreter's Bible,* XI, edited by Leander E. Keck, 469–549. Nashville: Abingdon, 2000.

Isasi-Díaz, Ada María. *La Lucha Continues: Mujerista Theology.* Maryknoll, NY: Orbis, 2004.

Jennings, Theodore. *Transforming Atonement: A Political Theology of the Cross.* Minneapolis: Fortress, 2009.

Johnson, Elizabeth. *Quest for the Living God: Mapping the Frontiers of the Theology of God.* New York: Continuum, 2007.

Kahl, Brigitte. *Galatians Re-Imagined: Reading with the Eyes of the Vanquished.* Minneapolis: Fortress, 2014.

————. "Galatians." In *Fortress Commentary on the Bible: The New Testament,* edited by Margaret Aymer, Cynthia Briggs Kittredge, and David Sanchez, 503–25. Minneapolis: Fortress, 2014.

King, Robert. *Thomas Merton and Thich Nhat Hanh: Engaged Spirituality in an Age of Globalization.* New York: Continuum, 2003.

Knitter, Paul. *Without Buddha I Could Not Be a Christian.* Trivandrum, India: Oneworld, 2009.

Kuruvilla, Carol. "Here's What Many White Christians Fail to Understand about The NFL Protest." https://www.huffingtonpost.com/entry/heres-what-many-white-christians-fail-to-understand-about-the-nfl-protests_us_59cbbd56e4b02aef6cd6a031?ncid=inblnkushpmg00000009.

Lathrop, Gordon. *Holy Ground: A Liturgical Cosmology.* Minneapolis: Fortress, 2003.

————. *Holy People: A Liturgical Ecclesiology.* Minneapolis: Fortress, 1999.

Levine, Amy-Jill. *Short Stories by Jesus: The Enigmatic Parables of a Controversial Rabbi.* New York: Harper Collins, 2014.

Lloyd, Vincent. *Black Natural Law.* New York: Oxford University Press, 2016.

Longnecker, Bruce. *The Triumph of Abraham's God: The Transformation of Identity in Galatians.* Nashville: Abingdon, 1998.

Lopez, Davina. *Apostle to the Conquered: Reimagining Paul's Mission.* Minneapolis: Fortress, 2010.

Lorde, Audre. *Sister Outsider: Essays and Speeches.* Berkeley, CA: Crossing, 2007.

McFarland, Ian. *The Divine Image: Envisioning the Invisible God.* Minneapolis: Fortress, 2005.

Myers, Ched, and Elaine Enns. *Ambassadors of Reconciliation: Volume I: New Testament Reflections on Restorative Justice and Peacemaking.* Maryknoll, NY: Orbis, 2009.

Nouwen, Henri. *The Wounded Healer.* New York: Doubleday, 1979.

Ottati, Douglas F. *Jesus Christ and Christian Vision.* Minneapolis: Fortress, 1989.

Park, Andrew Sung. *Triune Atonement: Christ's Healing for Sinners, Victims, and The Whole Creation.* Louisville: Westminster John Knox, 2009.

Powell, Mark Allan. "Generosity." In *The Dictionary of Scripture and Ethics,* edited by Joel Green, 324. Grand Rapids: Baker, 2011.

Rambo, Shelly. *Resurrecting Wounds: Living in the Afterlife of Trauma.* Waco, TX: Baylor University Press, 2017.

Reagan, Charles E. *Paul Ricoeur.* Chicago: University of Chicago Press, 1996.

Reid, Eric. "Why Colin Kaepernick and I Decided to Take a Knee." https://www. nytimes.com/2017/09/25/opinion/colin-kaepernick-football-protests. html?smprod=nytcore-ipad&smid=nytcore-ipad-share.

Rogers, Mary Beth. *Cold Anger: A Story of Faith and Power in Politics.* Denton, TX: University of North Texas Press, 1990.

Senior, Donald. *Why the Cross?* Nashville: Abingdon, 2014.

Shore-Goss, Robert. "An Ecological Reading of John 1 and Jesus as Gardener in His Encounter with Mary." In *Global Perspectives on the Bible,* edited by Mark Roncace and Joseph Weaver, 283–84. New York: Pearson Education, 2014.

St. Clair, Raquel A. *Call and Consequences: A Womanist Reading of Mark.* Minneapolis: Fortress, 2008.

Solberg, Mary M. "All That Matters: What an Epistemology of the Cross is Good For." In *Cross Examinations: Reading on the Meaning of the Cross Today,* edited by Marit Trelstad, 139–53. Minneapolis: Fortress, 2006.

Stevenson, Bryan. *Just Mercy: A Story of Redemption.* New York: Spiegel and Grau, 2014.

Sue, Derald Wing. *Microaggressions in Everyday Life: Race, Gender and Sexual Orientation.* Hoboken, NJ: John Wiley and Sons, 2010.

"Theology of Joy and the Good Life." http://faith.yale.edu/joy/about.

Thurman, Howard. *Jesus and the Disinherited.* Boston: Beacon,1976.

Tippett, Krista, and Ruby Sales. "Where Does It Hurt?" https://onbeing.org/ programs/ruby-sales-where-does-it-hurt-aug2017/.

Williams, Sam K. *Galatians.* Abingdon New Testament Commentaries. Nashville: Abingdon, 1997.

Wirzba, Norman. "Waking Up to the Anthropocene: Theological Resistance to Climate Change Paralysis." *Christian Century,* September 27, 2017, 22–27.

Wright, N. T. *The Day the Revolution Began: Reconsidering the Meaning of Jesus's Crucifixion.* San Francisco: HarperOne, 2016.

Volf, Miroslav. *A Public Faith: How Followers of Christ Should Serve the Common Good.* Grand Rapids: Brazos, 2011.